WORKING SCARED

WORKING SCARED

BLUEPRINTS FOR EMPLOYEES AND LEADERS
TO SUCCEED DURING TURBULENT TIMES

STANLEY B. SILVERMAN
KENNETH N. WEXLEY
DAVID H. WEXLEY

WILEY

Copyright © 2026 by John Wiley & Sons, Inc. All rights reserved, including rights for text and data mining and training of artificial intelligence technologies or similar technologies.

Published by John Wiley & Sons, Inc., Hoboken, New Jersey.

No part of this publication may be reproduced, stored in a retrieval system, or transmitted in any form or by any means, electronic, mechanical, photocopying, recording, scanning, or otherwise, except as permitted under Section 107 or 108 of the 1976 United States Copyright Act, without either the prior written permission of the Publisher, or authorization through payment of the appropriate per-copy fee to the Copyright Clearance Center, Inc., 222 Rosewood Drive, Danvers, MA 01923, (978) 750-8400, fax (978) 750-4470, or on the web at www.copyright.com. Requests to the Publisher for permission should be addressed to the Permissions Department, John Wiley & Sons, Inc., 111 River Street, Hoboken, NJ 07030, (201) 748-6011, fax (201) 748-6008, or online at http://www.wiley.com/go/permission.

The manufacturer's authorized representative according to the EU General Product Safety Regulation is Wiley-VCH GmbH, Boschstr. 12, 69469 Weinheim, Germany, e-mail: Product_Safety@wiley.com.

Trademarks: Wiley and the Wiley logo are trademarks or registered trademarks of John Wiley & Sons, Inc. and/or its affiliates in the United States and other countries and may not be used without written permission. All other trademarks are the property of their respective owners. John Wiley & Sons, Inc. is not associated with any product or vendor mentioned in this book.

Limit of Liability/Disclaimer of Warranty: While the publisher and the authors have used their best efforts in preparing this work, including a review of the content of the work, neither the publisher nor the authors make any representations or warranties with respect to the accuracy or completeness of the contents of this work and specifically disclaim all warranties, including without limitation any implied warranties of merchantability or fitness for a particular purpose. No warranty may be created or extended by sales representatives, written sales materials, or promotional statements for this work. The fact that an organization, website, or product is referred to in this work as a citation and/or potential source of further information does not mean that the publisher and authors endorse the information or services the organization, website, or product may provide or recommendations it may make. This work is sold with the understanding that the publisher is not engaged in rendering professional services. The advice and strategies contained herein may not be suitable for your situation. You should consult with a specialist where appropriate. Further, readers should be aware that websites listed in this work may have changed or disappeared between when this work was written and when it is read. Neither the publisher nor authors shall be liable for any loss of profit or any other commercial damages, including but not limited to special, incidental, consequential, or other damages.

For general information on our other products and services or for technical support, please contact our Customer Care Department within the United States at (800) 762-2974, outside the United States at (317) 572-3993 or fax (317) 572-4002.

Wiley also publishes its books in a variety of electronic formats. Some content that appears in print may not be available in electronic formats. For more information about Wiley products, visit our website at www.wiley.com.

Library of Congress Cataloging-in-Publication Data is Available:

ISBN 9781394387854 (Cloth)
ISBN 9781394387861 (ePub)
ISBN 9781394387878 (ePDF)

Cover Design: Wiley
Cover Image: © WonderPic/Getty Images
Author Photos: Courtesy of Stanley B. Silverman, Courtesy of Kenneth N. Wexley, Courtesy of David H. Wexley
Printed and bound by CPI Group (UK) Ltd, Croydon, CR0 4YY
C9781394387854_160326

This book is dedicated to our wonderful and supportive families.

Table of Contents

Preface — ix

Prologue: Stop Working Scared and Start Working Confidently — xi

1. Adapting to a Changing Workplace: Lessons from an AI Transformation — 1

2. Succeeding Amidst Arrogant Leadership: Steps to Succeed, Persist, and Protect Yourself — 25

3. Amplifying Your Voice in a Team Culture: How to Open Up Dialogue Even When It Feels Risky — 49

4. Thriving in a Hybrid Team: From the Office to Remote to Somewhere In-Between — 67

5. Enduring a Restructuring/Downsizing: Ways to Keep Your Job and Your Peace of Mind — 85

6. Prevailing Through Mergers and Acquisitions: Techniques to Face the Unknown and Find Your Place Again — 103

7. Building a Sense of Security Amidst Economic Turmoil: What to Do to Stay Grounded, Prepared, and Productive — 123

8. Prioritizing Personal Well-Being: The ROI of Taking Care of Yourself — 141

*Bringing It All Together: The Toolbox to Succeed
During Turbulent Times*   *155*
Appendix: The 10 Keys for Success Survey   *187*
Acknowledgments   *199*
The Authors   *199*
Notes   *203*
Index   *211*

Preface

We have been working as consultants to large and small organizations for several decades. During this time, we've had the pleasure of collaborating with and coaching leaders and employees at all levels, from the executive boardroom to the factory floor. In addition, we have held positions in academia and executive positions in large multinationals.

Lately, we've noticed a great unrest among employees in many organizations. At first, we thought that the unhappiness we were seeing was confined to a few unique companies. However, over time, we've come to realize that these feelings of uneasiness, fear, uncertainty, and worry are becoming pervasive globally. Several years ago, we began to refer to these feelings in the workplace as "working scared." We also noted that once employees begin working scared, they function less effectively in their jobs.

Why *This* Book

We believe this epidemic of fear is eating away at the core feelings and values of employees globally and that something had to be done. Inspired by our clients, our aim is to help employees and leaders who are working scared. Regardless of your position or tenure, you may be experiencing fear. You are not alone and this book is for you.

For the past few years, we've spoken with hundreds of workers who know this fear, either from their own experience or observing others who are working scared. Based on everything we have learned from them, plus our own consulting and business experience, we concluded that there are actions that employees and their leaders can take to cope with fear and achieve greater success. We've taken all these actions and put them into *Working Scared*.

A Real-World Perspective

Every incident described in this book is a real-world experience that we have personally observed or been told about. Nothing has been fabricated. For each chapter, we start off by giving you the facts about the issue so that you can get a feel for the importance of the topic. Next, we present a story – a *real* story. The only things we've changed are the names of the organizations and the individuals involved to safeguard their anonymity. Finally, we present actions and solutions that we have seen implemented successfully. The solutions are divided into two groups: those that are directed toward employees, and those that are directed to leaders.

The actions in each chapter are things you can apply immediately; tips to help employees cope with their own situations, and tips that leaders can use to help people become more successful.

Regardless of whether you're a leader or an employee, we highly recommend that you read both perspectives. Why? As a leader, don't forget that you are also an employee. And, as an employee, it pays for you to be knowledgeable about the kinds of things your manager can do for you. In fact, some of the actions that we suggest are things that you might pass along to your manager. We also realize that certain actions can help in many different situations. Rather than being redundant, we decided to place each in the one chapter where we felt it had the greatest benefit.

Prologue

Stop Working Scared and Start Working Confidently

"Working scared" has become a common reality for employees around the world. As markets shift and competition intensifies, organizations push harder to stay ahead. That pressure quickly cascades to individual employees, who face intensifying demands to perform. Those mounting expectations can feel overwhelming, creating fear and unease across all levels of the workplace.

Through our work with clients, we hear directly about the stress of today's workplace. In fact, we have experienced it ourselves. From these conversations and experiences, eight recurring themes of anxiety have emerged. Together with our clients, we have explored ways to address these challenges and developed practical actions that work. This book distills those lessons into a survival guide designed to help employees and leaders not only cope but also thrive in today's turbulent environment. Each of the eight themes forms a chapter and presents:

- Facts about the issue.
- A story of an employee who faced the situation.
- Proven actions for the employee and their manager – what employees can do to succeed in such a situation, and what

leaders can do to mitigate the fear in their teams so they can work more effectively.

In the subsequent chapters, we discuss:

1. **Adapting to a Changing Workplace.** Change is constant in every organization, now more than ever. Whether it's economic shifts, leadership transitions, new products, or evolving policies, adapting successfully requires commitment, skill, and focus. Successful organizations, teams, and individuals focus on building the capacity for change. When you, as an individual, aim for a clear goal and make steady progress toward it, you give yourself – and your team – the best chance at long-term success.

2. **Succeeding Amidst Arrogant Leadership.** Leadership shapes the culture of an organization. When leaders are perceived as being arrogant, it can drag down organizational performance and employee morale. Yet, arrogant leadership is becoming more prevalent. Confidence often propels individuals into leadership. But when that confidence becomes exaggerated, arrogance ensues, stifling others and hindering organizations. Greater awareness and behavioral adjustments can shift the dynamic toward a more constructive form of leadership.

3. **Amplifying Your Voice in a Team Culture.** Teams can survive without everyone contributing – but they don't thrive. The highest-performing teams make space for everyone to contribute fully. These teams are most cohesive, collaborative, innovative, and high performing over time. For team members to contribute, the team atmosphere must provide the encouragement, safety, and openness to welcome divergent voices.

4. **Thriving in a Hybrid Team.** Organizations are rethinking where and how we work. Traditional office life gave way to

remote work, and more recently, many teams are navigating hybrid models. Today, teams face a wide array of work arrangements. While the ingredients for effective teamwork remain the same – clear goals, strong collaboration, and open communication – the ways we work together, collaborate, and communicate have changed dramatically. As a result, we need to adapt how we connect and contribute to our organization.

5. **Enduring a Restructuring/Downsizing.** Restructuring is often driven by economic pressure – and it frequently means downsizing. These decisions are made at the organizational level – with long-term goals in mind, but they come with an immediate human cost. Whether you're one of the people leaving the organization, one of those who stay, or you're waiting to find out, the effects are felt deeply. But even during difficult transitions, there are opportunities to refocus and align one's efforts to capitalize on the change.

6. **Prevailing Through Mergers and Acquisitions.** Whether you follow business news or just hear it in passing, mergers and acquisitions are everywhere. These deals create entirely new organizations – and every person within them feels the impact. The workplace may look the same, but the dynamics, culture, and expectations often shift dramatically. After the M&A, it's not just *who* stays that matters, but *how* they align with the changes that come next.

7. **Building a Sense of Security Amidst Economic Turmoil.** These are turbulent times. Financial fluctuations, policy changes, and industry shifts create economic turmoil, putting pressure on organizations – and the people who work in them. When a company performs well, it can buffer some of that strain. But when it falters, employees often bear the brunt. That's why creating a sense of stability matters more than ever.

8. Prioritizing Personal Well-Being. Organizational performance depends on the well-being of its employees. When employees are healthy, they are more productive, more innovative, less absent, and more likely to stay with an organization. It therefore follows that organizations should prioritize the well-being of their employees. And yet, many fall short. That's why it's important for employees to take an active role in caring for their own well-being.

These areas of anxiety can trigger fear and even helplessness. Left unchecked, working scared undermines your ability to succeed on the job. Being scared isn't pleasant, but it is a natural human response. Fortunately, there are techniques to cope, and to succeed during today's turbulent times. That's what this book is all about. You will learn specific techniques you can use in each of the eight scenarios – and build better skills to help you navigate through *any* situation. First, let's find out what's happening in your work environment. Take a few minutes to complete the *Working Scared Survey* by answering each of the 50 questions below.

Working Scared Survey

	Never	Rarely	Sometimes	Often	Always
Adapting to a Changing Workplace					
My organization . . .					
1. . . . explains clearly what change means and encourages me to connect with it personally.					

	Never	Rarely	Sometimes	Often	Always
2. ... clarifies what meaningful goals I should pursue during times of change.					
3. ... provides meaningful feedback on my progress toward those goals.					
4. ... identifies whom I can reach out to for insight, support, and feedback during change.					
5. ... celebrates progress made toward achieving change-related goals.					
6. ... builds trust by helping employees feel less uncertain and vulnerable during change.					
7. ... fosters psychological safety by helping team members feel secure enough to take risks, speak up, or admit knowledge gaps.					

(continued)

	Never	Rarely	Sometimes	Often	Always
Succeeding Amidst Arrogant Leadership					
My organization . . .					
8. . . . reinforces that organizational objectives take priority over personal agendas.					
9. . . . emphasizes that feedback should be based on behaviors and results, not personal traits.					
10. . . . encourages leaders to listen to input before making decisions that impact others.					
11. . . . supports individuals in taking responsibility for both successes and failures.					
12. . . . ensures individuals understand their key responsibilities and the expectations within each of the key responsibilities.					

	Never	Rarely	Sometimes	Often	Always
13. ...upholds courtesy and respect in all interactions.					
Amplifying Your Voice in a Team Culture					
My organization . . .					
14. ...values and encourages speaking up.					
15. ...empowers individuals to share ideas, questions, concerns, or mistakes without fear of repercussions.					
16. ...invites new team members to contribute their voice.					
17. ...creates an environment where fear of speaking up is minimized.					
18. ...promotes a culture where every voice matters.					

(continued)

	Never	Rarely	Sometimes	Often	Always
19. . . . gives everyone space to contribute and model active listening.					
20. . . . acts on employee input when concerns or ideas are raised.					
Thriving in a Hybrid Team					
My organization . . .					
21. . . . embraces a flexible hybrid work model.					
22. . . . measures performance on outcomes rather than time at work.					
23. . . . strengthens team relationships so members feel accountable and committed to shared goals.					
24. . . . provides sufficient collaboration tools and the necessary training to increase connection.					

	Never	Rarely	Sometimes	Often	Always
25. ... establishes anchor days for in-office work.					
26. ... prioritizes team meetings during in-office days and conducts them to promote interaction.					
27. ... clarifies team norms and expectations to enhance communication and collaboration.					
Enduring a Restructuring/ Downsizing					
My organization . . .					
28. ... treats departing employees with respect during downsizing.					
29. ... provides extra support to remaining employees.					

(continued)

	Never	Rarely	Sometimes	Often	Always
30. . . . acknowledges feelings of sadness, role ambiguity, and caution during restructuring.					
31. . . . shares as much information as possible during restructuring.					
32. . . . encourages smart risk-taking after downsizing.					
33. . . . reinforces stability by clarifying new roles and expectations.					
Prevailing Through Mergers and Acquisitions					
My organization . . .					
34. . . . communicates regularly about the merger or acquisition.					
35. . . . highlights joint efforts between the merging organizations.					

	Never	Rarely	Sometimes	Often	Always
36. ... involves employees in integration activities (e.g., working groups, task forces, integration teams).					
37. ... provides opportunities for employees to share concerns and receive support.					
38. ... treats employees who leave during integration with dignity.					
39. ... clarifies how the merger or acquisition impacts employees' roles and career paths.					
Building a Sense of Security Amidst Economic Turmoil					
My organization . . .					
40. ... acknowledges uncertainty and creates open dialogue about economic challenges.					

(continued)

	Never	Rarely	Sometimes	Often	Always
41. . . . shares practical knowledge about persevering during economic and organizational turmoil.					
42. . . . reinforces structure and focus to help employees feel grounded.					
43. . . . reaffirms employees' value by linking their contributions to team and organizational success.					
44. . . . provides practical support related to financial stressors (e.g., student debt, lifestyle pressures).					
45. . . . communicates transparently about the organization's financial health and business outlook.					
Prioritizing Personal Well-Being					
My organization . . .					

	Never	Rarely	Sometimes	Often	Always
46. ... checks routinely on employees' well-being.					
47. ... shares information about healthy behaviors and discusses well-being openly.					
48. ... promotes healthy habits (e.g., vacations) and provides helpful resources (e.g., corporate wellness programs).					
49. ... provides flexible scheduling or workload adjustments to promote well-being.					
50. ... gives employees the feeling that they matter personally.					

Review your answers across the eight areas.

1. Wherever you selected "Never" or "Rarely," it signals that you may be working scared in that area.

2. Notice how many of the eight areas include one or more of these answers – this shows how widespread your fears may be, and where you may need to devote your attention.

Now that you have a clearer picture of your own situation, we'll guide you through the eight major sources of turbulence in today's workplace and the techniques that can help you succeed.

Chapter 1

Adapting to a Changing Workplace

Lessons from an AI Transformation

There is a familiar adage that "the only constant is change" – and these days, it seems change is accelerating. The way we work today would be unrecognizable to someone a generation ago, and we struggle to imagine what work will be like a generation from now. Change stems from evolving business needs, industry shifts, macroeconomic dynamics, and societal trends. Many of us are working scared because change frightens us. It triggers emotions and resistance that can hold us back from performing at our best.

Being able to manage change effectively is essential. Workplace changes fall into four broad categories:

1. **Structural changes** (such as reorganization or mergers)
2. **Operational changes** (like remote work and flexible schedules)
3. **Technological changes** (including automation, digital transformation, and artificial intelligence [AI])
4. **Cultural shifts** (factors related to leadership style, corporate culture, and values)

Throughout this book, we will cover specific changes in each of these four categories that can trigger fear. This chapter, as a starting point, provides a general resource for dealing with these changes – and *any change* – you may encounter. You can use the techniques for yourself, in your one-on-one relationships, or when working in a team.

Let's Look at Some Facts

- **Change is accelerating:** nearly two-thirds of employees have experienced increased workplace change in the past year.[1]
- **Change is becoming more extreme:** the average employee underwent 10 planned enterprise changes in 2022, such as restructuring or technology replacements. That was a fivefold increase from just seven years earlier.[2]
- **Change is disruptive:** 70% of US workers reported disruptive change in their organization. 20% cited a large or very large change ranging from restructuring to shifting return-to-office expectations. These changes have a noticeable impact on employees' performance. Employees who experience disruptive change are less engaged and more likely to leave their job.[3]
- **Change requires learning new skills:** 85% of employers surveyed plan to prioritize upskilling their workforce, with 70% of employers expecting to hire staff with new skills, and 40% planning to reduce staff as their skills become less relevant.[4]

Think about the difficult changes that have taken place in your workplace. How many of them did you initiate? How many of them did you help shape? How many were simply imposed on you? Chances are, most of them felt beyond your control. We make a distinction between *change* and *choice*. For example, you might choose to switch jobs and feel excited about the opportunity. However, if you were suddenly reassigned to that same role, you might feel anxious instead. Why does one situation feel liberating while the other feels constraining? Because we typically resist change – even a positive one – when it is imposed on us, yet we embrace it when it's a choice. Change typically comes from outside; choice comes from within. People want to be involved in shaping change: *change as a choice rather than as a condition*. When employees have choices in the change, they are more likely to support it. Gaining some autonomy is not only a way to contribute to change, but an effective way of managing the fear that may come from it.

In this chapter, you will learn a practical technique that helps individuals and teams navigate change more effectively. The approach creates opportunities to make choices along the way. By engaging fully in the process, you can lessen the fear of change and capitalize on its opportunities.

Janice's Story

Janice is a product manager at a global pharmaceutical company. She has a successful track record marked by steady progress up in the organization. She and her team are responsible for product strategy, including planning, development, and commercialization of new pharmaceutical products. When she started at the company nearly 25 years ago, it was already a well-established player in a fragmented domestic market. Since then, her company has grown, consolidated with competitors, and expanded internationally. Today, she works as part of a global team with colleagues

(continued)

(continued)
doing research and development in France, Japan, and Mexico. Janice still loves her job, her company, and the industry – but lately, she's been feeling unsettled.

> *"Honestly, I'm kind of overwhelmed,"* she admitted. *"Everyone's talking about Artificial Intelligence (AI). It seems like there's a new AI initiative every few weeks. One day it's using AI to optimize clinical trials, the next day it's for automating regulatory submissions, or to engage with customers. I feel like I can't keep up – and I'm worried if I don't, I'll be left behind."*

Adding to her concern, her company recently announced a large investment in AI capabilities, spearheaded by the new Chief Technology Officer. The CTO has little experience in pharmaceuticals, having been recruited from a leading tech firm. Janice felt the leadership in her company was sending a clear message: AI will be integrated across the business, from R&D to marketing to medical affairs. Teams were asked to identify opportunities for automation, and much of the internal communications stressed the company's intended leadership in what they hailed as the "AI transformation of big pharma."

At first, Janice tried to keep an open mind. She attended a few AI-focused lunch-and-learn sessions and experimented with a newly launched tool designed to generate insights by analyzing patient data. Her head spun each time she entered this unfamiliar world. The more she heard, the more concerned she became. *"I don't know why everything suddenly must be driven by AI. We've been successful for years because of our deep scientific knowledge and collaboration. It feels like they want to replace our human expertise with a bunch of machine algorithms."*

Then, suddenly the changes became real. Several roles in her division were redefined or eliminated, with some of the more repetitive functions, like data synthesis, report generation, and even early drafts of slide decks, now being handled by AI-powered platforms. Her manager, a trusted mentor for four years, was offered a different position in the organization. Janice would now report to a newly appointed leader, named Marta, who had a background predominantly in data science, not pharmaceuticals.

Adopting AI became a strategic priority. The executive team framed AI as a competitive differentiator: adopt it and thrive or become irrelevant. Leaders began linking productivity gains to AI adoption, citing the enormous cost savings that AI could generate for shareholders. AI readiness was quickly becoming the new performance standard that everyone was expected to meet. The team was feeling the pressure.

Looking around at her extended team, Janice noticed that many of her younger colleagues seemed comfortable experimenting with AI tools. They used AI for tasks like creating project updates, tracking of Key Performance Indicators (KPIs), and drafting customer communications. The things that had always required Janice's deep expertise and hours of effort could now be done by junior team members in a fraction of the time. *"They seem to pick it up so fast,"* she thought. *"And I have to admit, their work is really impressive."*

At lunch with her long-time colleagues, the sense of uneasiness was palpable. They discussed whether their tasks would be automated, and if their jobs would be eliminated. Team goals were

(continued)

(continued)
in flux, and their roles were becoming less clear. Even the team's sense of shared purpose, something Janice had always cherished, felt diluted.

As the changes accelerated, Janice found it harder to concentrate. She was distracted by announcements, unsure of how to contribute, and increasingly worried about whether her hard-earned experience still mattered. She felt this change was being *imposed on her*. She wasn't against change, but she just didn't feel part of it. As her confidence diminished, so did her optimism about her future with the company and in the industry she loved. She couldn't deny that she was working scared in the face of a seismic shift.

Janice reminded herself that she had navigated big changes before. When she entered the industry in the early 1990s, there wasn't even email. She chuckled when she thought of all the hype around the dot-com boom. She remembered embracing that change wholeheartedly. Since then, there have been numerous shifts in her industry: globalization, regulatory reform, and new technologies. Each time, she had adapted. Was this so different? In these moments, a tinge of curiosity slipped into her head. What if some of the AI tools could help her be more effective? What if AI would bring something meaningful to her industry? Was there a way to view this change as an opportunity and help shape it like she had previous changes? She hoped so, but wasn't yet sure how to do it.

Actions for Employees

An important technique for managing the fear of change is gaining clarity on where the change is leading, why it is important, and what your contribution is. In the workplace, many of us might feel that change is done *to* us, rather than being done *with* us. To respond confidently rather than react, start by asking yourself what the change truly means and what you want to achieve from it. Then consider how you will adapt – how you might shift your mindset, expand your capabilities, and adjust your behaviors to meet new demands. As you progress over time, it is important to take stock and recognize even small steps forward, as these signal genuine adaptation to the change. Finally, look for ways to build on that momentum, gradually increasing your efforts as your confidence grows. Keep in mind that behavioral change takes time and intention, but each progressive step expands your capacity for change.

The philosophy described above is captured in a framework we have used with clients for years called the AIME Model for Change. AIME stands for *Align, Integrate, Monitor,* and *Elevate*. We have used it to help our clients – including Janice and her team – orient themselves and their teams toward change. AIME works whether the change is a small shift in a team or a massive industry-wide disruption. The AIME Model helps you to *aim toward a desired outcome and supports you along the way*. It encompasses four steps:

- **Align:** "What's a meaningful goal for me in this change?"
- **Integrate:** "What behaviors or perspectives move me closer to my goal?"
- **Monitor:** "What signs of progress toward my goal do I notice?"
- **Elevate:** "What could be next for me now that I've made some progress?"

Let's explore these four steps in more detail and how they helped Janice navigate change more effectively.

ALIGN with *Your Goal*

Change – especially when it's unexpected – can shake our sense of stability and control. We may perceive the situation as a threat. Our first (natural) instinct may be to resist it, hoping things will return to the familiar. But, in many cases, the decision to change is already in motion and beyond our control. Rather than staying stuck in opposition, **Aligning** is the first active choice you can make. It's not about blind acceptance; it's about finding your place within the change and *choosing* how you want to engage with it.

To align is to step back and ask *what is meaningful for you here and what you want to move toward*. When you connect to a goal that matters personally – whether it's developing new skills, preserving key relationships, or seeking out a new opportunity – you begin to anchor yourself in a purpose within the context of the broader change taking place around you.

Helpful questions to consider include:

- How does the change impact you?
- What opportunities – large or small – does the change create?
- How can you contribute in a way that aligns with your values and perspective?
- And finally, what is **your goal** in this change; how do you align yourself with it?

In our work with Janice, this step took time and several iterations. Initially, she took an oppositional stance toward all the change. She spoke skeptically about the direction new leadership was taking and struggled to see how she could support, or even fit into, the change. In our sessions, we returned repeatedly to the core questions of the Align stage: *How does this change impact you? What opportunities could it hold?* Over time, Janice's thinking began to shift. She acknowledged that new leadership and the move toward AI might introduce fresh insights and learning opportunities – something she realized she hadn't actively pursued in recent years. She also recognized that cultural shift toward AI was still taking shape, and with her deep institutional knowledge, she was uniquely positioned to help blend the best of the old with promising aspects of the new. By shifting her mindset from resistance to curiosity, Janice was able to realign herself with the change – not with passive acceptance, but by identifying a meaningful role she could play in shaping it. We encouraged her to discuss her new insights openly with her manager, Marta.

As we did with Janice, we recommend you take your time with this step. *Don't rush it.* Write down your goals, revisit them, and adjust them if necessary. The more you do this, the more alignment you will likely find between your goals and the broader organizational ones. Furthermore, having them written down as a handy reference can serve as a stabilizer in a disorienting situation.

INTEGRATE Productive Thoughts and Behaviors

The second step in AIME is to **Integrate** thoughts and behaviors that move you toward the goal – and to shift or change those that move you away. This is where reflection becomes action. Think of this phase as putting the puzzle pieces together: integrating your mindset, skills, habits, and support systems to adapt to the change and move you closer to your goal. Begin by asking: *Are my current thoughts, reactions, and behaviors helping or hindering my progress?*

During this phase, you will identify how to:

- **Adjust your mindset** by reframing the change as an opportunity rather than a threat. How can you shift your perspective to better embrace the change and uncover its opportunities?

- **Identify skill gaps** that may hold you back and consider ways to build new capabilities. What are you doing that is helpful? What are you doing that's counterproductive? What new behaviors, routines, or conversations can help you gain momentum?
- **Build up your resources** including people in your network who can offer ideas, encouragement, guidance, and practical support. Who can you reach out to for insight, support, feedback, or just to challenge your thinking?
- **Incorporate** new habits and behaviors into your daily work routines that align with your goal.

This is often a creative and energizing phase. You're not just coping with change; you are *designing how you will integrate it*. To broaden your thinking, speak with trusted colleagues, mentors, friends, and other people in your network who might have a unique perspective. The simple act of generating constructive ideas – rather than venting frustrations – can help shift your energy, reinforce your motivation, and make the change feel more manageable. Integration means deciding for yourself what to carry forward, what to let go of, and what new patterns to adopt.

As Janice worked on the Integrate phase of AIME, she began translating her newly clarified goals into practical strategies. Janice acknowledged a need to learn about external technology trends impacting her industry and to expand her own knowledge to better understand them. She had enjoyed the lunch-and-learns and was pleasantly surprised how much she understood how AI might help the business. Now was the time to accelerate her learning. She saw the opportunity to leverage her well-established industry expertise to explore new data insights, market opportunities, and delivery models. She set a goal to position herself as someone who could combine her existing expertise with new AI insights to help shape the evolution of her company.

With those goals in mind, Janice integrated new thoughts and behaviors that would move her forward. As a product manager, she recognized her skills as a strategist – a structured thinker who understands why businesses need to continuously evolve. At the same time, she realized that many of her conversations about the change were confined to a small circle of familiar colleagues who echoed her skepticism. These discussions, while comfortable, were not helping her progress. So, Janice made a conscious choice to engage more broadly. She began having targeted conversations with others across the organization. She also asked Marta for advice on how she herself was integrating new thinking into her work.

Although the topic initially felt intimidating, Janice reframed it as a learning opportunity and a concrete way to move closer to her goal. She accelerated her learning on how AI would impact the pharmaceutical industry. She read articles and chatted with a neighbor with some knowledge of the field. She enrolled in a four-week online course called "Intro to AI for Business Professionals." It took just a couple of hours a week, but she found the lectures and discussions with other students insightful, inspiring – and reassuring. This was a clear example of integration: she addressed a skill gap, expanded her network, and adopted new behaviors that shifted her mindset toward shaping the change, all in alignment with her personal goals.

MONITOR and Acknowledge Progress

The third step in the AIME model is to **Monitor** your progress. In times of change, the end goal can feel far off. Therefore, it becomes especially important to pause, look for signs of movement, and recognize momentum. Progress can be tangible, like influencing a key decision, completing a course, or receiving recognition from peers. But it is often intangible – like feeling more optimistic, gaining a greater sense of control, or shifting from skepticism to curiosity. These intangible signs of progress are often overlooked but acknowledging them can be highly motivating.

Consider questions such as:

- What are the tangible and intangible signs of progress?
- What hurdles have you encountered, and how have you responded?
- How is your effort today different from how you might have responded a month ago?
- How can you celebrate the steps you've made?

Monitoring helps reinforce your commitment to the goal. Even small wins can boost motivation and enhance resilience.

For Janice, the Monitor stage was about noticing shifts – both in her external actions and in her internal stance toward the change. After expanding her network and starting to explore AI in pharmaceutical development, she noticed a shift in her mindset. Instead of feeling dread, she felt a growing curiosity. She noted that her conversations had become more constructive and forward-looking. These were not things she would have celebrated in the past – but in this context, they were clear signs of progress.

Tangible indicators emerged as well. Her manager, Marta, was supportive and encouraging. She nominated Janice to represent the team in a cross-functional working group focused on an AI-enabled application. She also began drafting a short internal memo to keep the broader team up to date on the activities of the working group. The personal work Marta was doing to embrace change was now helping others in the organization to successfully do the same. A couple of colleagues sent her messages of appreciation. These moments, small as they seemed, gave Janice confidence that she was on the right track. By taking time to reflect on them, she stayed motivated, reminded herself of how far she had come, and reinforced her commitment to the goals she had set during the Align phase.

ELEVATE Efforts to Build on Success

As we stated at the beginning of this chapter, the only constant is change. Therefore, the AIME framework includes a fourth step, **Elevate**, which involves building on the progress you've made and using it as a springboard for greater impact. Change doesn't end with initial adaptation; it unfolds over time. Elevation is about expanding your efforts, deepening your commitment to the change, and perhaps even helping others navigate their own change journeys.

During this phase, ask:

- How can you build on your progress?
- How can you level-up your efforts – or even scale them to benefit others?
- What new goals are you ready to pursue?
- How can you contribute to the broader direction of change?

In an organizational context, to elevate is to shift from managing change to helping shape it. Reaching this stage helps reinforce your sense of control and enhances your change agility. The more you elevate your response to change, the more resilient and future-ready you become.

For Janice, the Elevate stage came into focus when she made a bold choice: she put her name forward to serve on the company's Advisory Committee for the AI initiative. Just months earlier, she had been resistant, unsure if she even wanted to stay at the company. Now, she was stepping into a visible role – helping guide the very transformation she once doubted. This move allowed Janice not only to build on her personal progress, but also to shape the change on a broader scale. Her institutional knowledge and broad industry perspective made her a valued voice on the committee. For Janice, elevation wasn't about ambition for its own sake, but rather it was about continuing the step-by-step journey she had begun with AIME: aligning with her meaningful purpose, integrating new behaviors, monitoring her progress, and ultimately elevating her capacity to lead in change.

The AIME Model for Change is designed to guide you over time. Think of it as a framework you return to for support as circumstances shift or new challenges arise. You may find yourself moving back and forth between steps – realigning, reintegrating, monitoring, and elevating – rather than following them in a straight line. Each time, you will gain deeper insights. This flexibility is what makes our Model so practical. It provides structure and reassurance, helping you stay on track through the ups and downs of change.

**Adapting to a Changing Workplace:
The Blueprint for Employees**

- Acknowledge the emotions that change triggers
- Use the AIME Model for Change to guide your efforts toward a meaningful goal
  - A = ALIGN efforts toward *your goal*
  - I = INTEGRATE productive thoughts and behaviors
  - M = MONITOR and acknowledge progress
  - E = ELEVATE efforts to build on success
- Revisit the AIME Model regularly to stay on track

Actions for Leaders

During times of change, your leadership plays a pivotal role in shaping how employees respond – whether they actively resist, passively disengage, or contribute constructively. Reducing fear and uncertainty does not require having all the answers or a perfect plan. It means creating conditions where your employees feel supported and empowered to act. As a leader, it's important to view change readiness not only as a mindset but as a skill set – one that can be strengthened through guidance, feedback, and practice. The strategies below will help you to do that. They include using the AIME Model for Change in your coaching conversations and complementary techniques that are designed to amplify the benefits of the AIME framework. Used together, these techniques will help you foster the mindset and environment in which employees can align with change, integrate new ways of thinking and working, monitor their progress, and ultimately elevate their contribution. As a leader, your role is to create space for authentic dialogue, to role model adaptability, and to offer practical support where possible. The actions that follow are a practical approach to bringing these foundational elements to life in your everyday leadership.

Use the AIME Model to Coach

Once Janice was familiar with the AIME framework, she introduced it to Marta. Together, they used it to orient Janice's efforts toward the changes taking place in their company and across the industry. While Marta's background was in data science and she had some AI experience, she admitted to Janice that at times even she was unsure where things were headed. She acknowledged that the AIME Model helped her to stay change ready and to better guide the team.

The AIME framework provides a useful structure to reduce your employees' fear of change and increase engagement. Each step of AIME offers a natural opening for dialogue:

- **A**lign: "What's a meaningful goal for you in this change?"
- **I**ntegrate: "What new behaviors or perspectives could move you closer?"
- **M**onitor: "What signs of progress are you noticing?"
- **E**levate: "What could be next for you now that you've made some progress?"

Through AIME, you can help your employees move from being passive recipients of change to active participants in shaping their own experience.

But, for AIME to have lasting impact, these conversations must be supported by a broader leadership environment that bolsters trust, creates space for dialogue, fosters psychological safety, models authenticity, and celebrates small wins. The actions that follow offer specific ways to create just that kind of environment.

Treat Adaptability as a Skill Set

Change readiness is not a fixed trait. Rather it should be viewed the same way you view any job-related skill – something that can be developed, strengthened, and evaluated over time. As a leader, treat adaptability as a core competency by building it into how you hire, develop, manage, and motivate your team. Ask questions about past change experiences. Clarify specific behaviors that reflect change readiness – such as curiosity, resilience, or willingness to experiment – and include them in development plans and performance reviews. Encourage stretch projects that build change capacity, and provide regular coaching, support, and feedback. Reward examples that demonstrate growth. When you treat change like a trainable skill, your team will learn to change – and better performance will follow.

Bolster Trust

Trust is the foundation of adaptive behavior. During change, employees often feel uncertain and vulnerable – which can erode trust and lead to rigid thinking. In such situations, you need to enhance trust to help reduce this anxiety. Trust doesn't mean having all the answers. Rather, it means being transparent, following through on your commitments, and being empathetic. When you establish a solid basis of trust, your employees will be more willing to explore new directions and engage in the change constructively using a framework like AIME.

Marta, who had only recently joined the company, focused on building trust with her team. In Janice, she appreciated someone with deep industry and institutional knowledge. She saw their strengths as complementary. In her meetings with Janice, she conveyed how much she appreciated that they had different skill sets that made their team stronger. Each could learn from the other, and by acknowledging her own limitations, Marta made it safe for Janice to do the same. Their relationship evolved from a solid basis of trust.

Create Space for Dialogue

Change is emotional, and people need space to process it. You can support your employees by intentionally creating space for dialogue, where your team feels safe to ask questions, raise concerns, and express their emotions. Do not rush to fix or dismiss resistance; rather listen actively and with empathy. These open conversations often become the starting point for Align, helping employees articulate what is meaningful to them amid uncertainty.

Marta started every team meeting with updates from each team member. She encouraged people to share openly – even if it meant airing their concerns about the changes taking place. She noticed that starting each meeting this way kept people engaged and encouraged the team to support each other through the uncertain times.

Foster Psychological Safety

Psychological safety – where team members feel secure enough to take risks, speak up, or admit gaps in knowledge – is essential for employees to try new behaviors and experiment with change.[5] Remember that change is often met with fear and a sense of danger, pushing people to revert to old habits. Your job is to increase the sense of security by fostering psychological safety. Encourage diverse perspectives, show appreciation for candor, and reward smart risk-taking. Meanwhile, role model vulnerability by admitting mistakes, describing your own uncertainties, and sharing your personal experiences with change. AIME thrives in environments where it is safe to think out loud, stumble occasionally, and learn iteratively.

In their one-on-one meetings, Marta reiterated her admiration for how Janice was trying to enhance her existing expertise by bolstering her understanding of AI. In one meeting, Marta told her, given the pace of change, *"nobody is going to get it right 100% of the time."* Marta encouraged her to take some calculated risks; she trusted her and told her she was ready to support her decisions. She gave Janice the psychological safety to learn and admit mistakes if they occurred.

Model Authenticity

Employees don't need you to be perfect, they need you to be authentic. When leaders share their own uncertainties or their learning needs during change, they signal that it is okay not to have everything figured out. Authentic leadership builds connection and trust, while also modeling the Integrate and Monitor stages of AIME. For example, a leader who says, *"I've been trying to adapt and to learn myself. What's helped me is . . ."* sets an example on how to integrate new behaviors and creates permission for others to be vulnerable and engage constructively.

Marta found opportunities to do this in her team meetings and one-on-ones. Given her own career path, she freely admitted that she had a lot to learn about the pharmaceuticals industry. She was confident in her AI knowledge but acknowledged that tapping into AI opportunities at the intersection of AI and pharma needed the collective wisdom of her skilled team of experts. Janice genuinely appreciated Marta's authenticity.

Celebrate Small Wins

Change is difficult. Small wins sometimes go unnoticed and are usually unacknowledged. In the uncertainty of organizational change, progress can feel invisible. Leaders who observe, name, and celebrate small wins reinforce a culture of successful change and growth. As a leader, you may notice a subtle mindset shift, an employee's willingness to try a new behavior, or their ability to navigate uncertainty with greater confidence. These small steps fuel motivation and resilience. While Key Performance Indicators (KPIs) are essential for tracking the substantive outcomes of change, they don't always capture the small behavioral shifts that make change possible. Therefore, we encourage people to also look to tiny behavioral improvements, which we have named **micro-Performance Indicators** *("mPIs")*. An mPI is a small meaningful change in behavior that contributes to a new habit, interaction, or a greater goal. Acknowledging these tiny steps forward helps to sustain progress. We provide a more detailed overview of mPI in the Appendix at the end of this chapter, which explains how you can use the concept in your teams. Celebrating small wins ties directly to the Monitor phase and keeps energy high through the long arc of transformation.

Marta encouraged Janice to reflect on her progress. She asked Janice, *"since the AI initiative was launched, what's something you're proud of?"* Janice talked about the efforts she made in her learning journey. Then Marta pressed a little further; *"great, what else?"* At first, Janice was embarrassed to admit it, but then she said she made a conscious effort not to complain with her friends about the change. After doing this, she started to notice that she had greater feelings of optimism and confidence. Marta said, *"That's an important success that we sometimes fail to see. So, I'm glad to hear you recognize that mPI."* In this exchange, Marta demonstrated how to use mPI to keep Janice motivated and on track.

You do not need formal training to use the actions we outlined in this chapter. You just need to create space for dialogue, build trust, ask thoughtful questions, and show your employees empathy and commitment. These foundational behaviors can go a long way in helping employees to stop working scared during change, and to find their way forward during turbulent times.

Adapting to a Changing Workplace: The Blueprint for Leaders

- Create space to process
- Explain and reiterate the rationale
- Apply the AIME Model for Change to guide and support
- Treat adaptability as a skill set – and train your team to change
- Foster psychological safety
- Be a consistent and stabilizing force
- Communicate transparently
- Use micro-Performance Indicators (mPIs) to acknowledge and celebrate small steps in progress

Appendix: Explanation of a micro-Performance Indicator ("mPI")

Why Is This Important?

In our roles as leaders, we are trained to see the big things, such as major milestones or breakthroughs in a change process. The notion of KPIs is built on that. We encourage you to do something different: to notice small, meaningful steps along the way. We call these mPIs, *micro-Performance Indicators*.

What Is an mPI?

An mPI is defined as "a small meaningful change in behavior that contributes to a new habit, interaction, or greater goal." They emerge in one's own behavior, or they can be observed in others. An mPI surfaces as an impression, feeling, sensation, or experience. It is a subjective and qualitative measure of progress, but one that can serve as a basis for reflection and discussion. mPIs are typically formulated in a simple sentence, like "I noticed lately a small improvement in . . .." The act of acknowledging small steps reinforces and motivates ongoing behavioral change.

Where Do They Occur?

An mPI can occur in an individual, team, or at an organizational level. However, the concept was developed to reflect on team performance that is predicated on healthy interaction. Although there are no predefined rules of where an mPI occurs, they often emerge in:

- How we **relate to and interact with others**
- How effectively we complete our **work**

- Our **sense of identity**
- Our **mindset, attitude, and outlook**

When and How Do You Find mPIs?

Once you are oriented toward mPIs, they are easier to notice. Once noticed, they are easier to reinforce. As a leader, we encourage you to discuss mPIs in your interactions with your team members.

Collect mPIs in any manner that is convenient. Feel free to jot them down on a notepad, send yourself an email, record a voice memo, or capture a picture representing the mPI.

We encourage you to bring the concept of mPIs into your team and invite them to share what they notice. Drawing others into the practice of noticing small changes is a powerful way of reinforcing behaviors that will contribute to achieving your team goals.

Examples of mPIs:
- I now look forward to our team meetings. People seem to ask more questions, there's a better exchange of ideas, and it feels like we resolve issues better
- The office seems to be filled with more energy than before
- We are more proactive and innovative in solving problems
- I have a better sense of our overarching team goals and how I can contribute
- When my manager checks in on me, it feels more encouraging and supportive than before

If we only used KPIs to track performance improvements, these small behavioral shifts would likely go unnoticed. Therefore, the concept of mPI is meant to complement KPIs to get a broader sense of progress – capturing large-scale, quantitative metrics with

KPIs while acknowledging the many small, qualitative improvements through mPIs.

Comparison of KPI and mPI

	KPI **Key Performance Indicator**	**mPI** **micro-Performance Indicator**
Definition	Indicators that focus on the aspects of organizational performance that are the most critical for the current and future success of the organization	Small meaningful changes in behavior that contribute to a new habit, interaction, or greater goal. They occur at an individual, team, or organization level
Selection	Set top-down and changed infrequently	Emerge bottom-up and evolve organically
Number	Very few	Limitless
Measurement	Quantitative At regular intervals	Qualitative As they emerge
Motivation	To encourage action	To reinforce behavior
Impact	Link behavior to critical success factors	Link behavior to critical success factors

Adapting to a Changing Workplace

Chapter 2

Succeeding Amidst Arrogant Leadership

Steps to Succeed, Persist, and Protect Yourself

"How many of you have ever worked for someone you consider to be arrogant?" We have given presentations throughout the United States and Europe and when we ask the question, most of the audience raised their hands! The news and business periodicals are peppered with stories of executives flying in private jets while asking for government handouts, taking large bonuses from employers who took billions in bailout money. In addition, many were instigating downsizing practices, organization-wide pay cuts, and benefit rollbacks while keeping themselves immune from such changes. Indeed, we have been operating in an "age of arrogance"[1] and we clearly are still today.

Let's Look at Some Facts

Our research, which is cited in this chapter, has resulted in the only measure of workplace arrogance, and indicates that a consequence of arrogant leadership is employee fear. Their fear manifests as counterproductive emotions. According to Gallup's workforce indicators on employee well-being from February 2025, 52% of US workers report feeling a lot of stress, 44% report feeling a lot of worry, 24% report feeling a lot of sadness, and 22% report feeling a lot of anger.[2]

Beyond Self-Confidence

We define **arrogance** as a stable attitude of superiority and an exaggerated sense of self-confidence. It can be thought of as a cluster of behaviors that communicate one's superiority and importance relative to others.[3] We have no problem working for leaders who are self-confident, but when they cross the line to being overly self-confident, they become arrogant. Arrogant leaders can be an especially challenging problem to deal with because they consider their behavior acceptable and therefore do not change these behaviors when interacting with others. Where does arrogance come from? Often, leaders think things are clear. They've often been in the role for a long time, and they might think success is clearly defined. Typically, it isn't.

What Are Some Consequences of Arrogant Leadership?

Notes from the field. We have developed a measure of workplace arrogance. The corresponding research is cited in this chapter. The results have been summarized in magazines, newspapers, and online publications all over the world. It is clear, from the results of our research, that leader arrogance has led to lower productivity, lower morale and job satisfaction, and higher burnout among employees.

- The research shows that arrogant leaders place little value on other people's ideas, input, and feedback, claim to be more knowledgeable than others, and sometimes publicly belittle and disparage others to exaggerate their own self-importance. Additionally, even though their behaviors appear to express their inflated self-concepts, such behaviors are unwarranted, as these individuals tend to exhibit lower self-esteem, cognitive ability, and job performance.[4] According to those surveyed in 2025, 75% of why people quit comes down to their leader/manager.[5]

- According to a 2025 survey, 51% of employees are actively seeking new opportunities – the highest rate in over a decade.[6] We believe that one of the major reasons employees are seeking new opportunities is largely due to their leader's behavior, including arrogance. Nearly one-third of Americans said they directly experienced abusive behavior at work.[7]

- We should keep in mind that arrogance occurs on a continuum in the sense that there are varying degrees of arrogance (to measure arrogance, we have developed the Workplace Arrogance Scale that appears in the Appendix at the end of this chapter). It is important to understand that to be perceived as being an arrogant leader one does not need to be rated high on all the items, just some of them.

- The more arrogant an individual leader is perceived to be, the more their employees believe that the individual:
  - shoots down other people's ideas in public
  - puts personal agenda ahead of organizational objectives
  - willingly takes credit for success but not blame for failure
  - does not welcome constructive feedback
  - gets angry when their ideas are criticized
  - displays unwillingness to listen to others' opinions, ideas, or perspectives

- Our research has shown[8] that high leader arrogance has been empirically linked to:
  - Lower leader job performance
  - Lower leader cognitive ability
  - Lower leader self-esteem
- Our research has also shown[9] that employees who have more arrogant leaders:
  - Rate their feedback environment less favorably
  - Report engaging in less feedback seeking
  - Experience lower levels of morale and job satisfaction
  - Experience higher levels of burnout
- Here are some interesting things to think about:
  - Are arrogant leaders actually superior? No, they often mistakenly believe they are just self-confident
  - Arrogant behaviors may be a façade to mask feelings of incompetence or low self-confidence
  - Arrogant leaders find it difficult to accept criticism and often rely on sycophantic advisors who tell them what they want to hear
  - Arrogant leaders may be overly optimistic concerning the possibility of success – often disregarding competition allowing them to become complacent
  - Often employees do not leave organizations – they leave managers. Organizations need to find ways to soften the impact of arrogant leaders and work on their development
- Are arrogant bosses causing employees to work scared? You bet! Simply put, the effect of arrogant leaders is scared employees.

Megan's Story

Megan works for a large corporation that is a manufacturer of hand-held computers. These computers are sold to two main types of customers: restaurant chains, where they are used by servers when taking food and beverage orders, and retail establishments, such as department stores and clothing stores, for inventory control. Last year, their sales and customer service division reorganized, and one management layer was eliminated. A year ago, there were three levels of management separating the vice president of sales and customer service from the customer success representatives. Then, the corporation eliminated a layer of management. Before the reorganization, five supervisors reported to each regional manager. Today all 20 of these supervisors report directly to the company's director of customer service. Megan is one of the 20 supervisors who now report directly to Terry, the director of customer service. Up until last year, Megan met every week with the regional manager she reported to; these weekly meetings gave Megan direction, feedback, and a feeling of security. If she made a mistake, her last manager would always turn it into a learning opportunity. She doesn't have the same close working relationship with Terry. Megan realizes that different leaders have different styles, but Terry, at times, seems to look for ways to criticize Megan's actions. He often acts as if he knows better than everyone else, and puts his personal agenda ahead of the organization's agenda. She has observed him discredit others' ideas during meetings. Terry comes across as arrogant, unlike anyone that she has worked with in the past. Megan is working scared.

(continued)

(continued)

In a recent meeting with Terry, Megan discussed her department. She left the session feeling anxious about her future at the company. For one thing, Megan found that she and Terry had very different ideas about what she is expected to accomplish. Megan was upset when Terry angrily informed her that she needed to keep him more informed about customer complaints. This was particularly distressing because Megan felt she had been doing a good job keeping Terry informed. Megan left the meeting feeling that she was in a no-win situation. After talking to several of her colleagues, she realized that she wasn't the only one on the receiving end of Terry's arrogant behaviors. Often, he is willing to take credit for his department's successes but seldom is willing to admit a mistake. She realizes that he is busy, but at the same time, she does not appreciate the way he sometimes treats her and her peers, and the inappropriate ways he gives them feedback. She wants to do a better job but doesn't understand what Terry wants her to do differently. In short, Megan wants Terry's help to develop in her role but realizes that he often seems more interested in his own personal agenda.

Megan learns that the organization is doing a 360° feedback process with all leaders at Terry's level and above. She is hoping that this process may give Terry the anonymous feedback that he needs.

Why Is Arrogance in Leadership So Prevalent? There Are Three Major Traps

- **Self-perception:** Many leaders overestimate their knowledge. They like to think of themselves as the smartest person in the room even though they rarely are.

- **Outside expectations:** High performance expectations put on leaders continues to increase (e.g., greater span of control), which means managers have less time to spell out clear expectations for their employees.
- **Control issues:** Many leaders thrive on power. They may hold on to information as a source of power, while keeping others – especially their team members – ill-informed.

Leaders who fall into one or more of these traps may be perceived as arrogant. Whatever the source of the behavior, *employees* need ways to mitigate the effects of a leader's arrogant behavior.

The number of direct reports has been increasing steadily across all industries since 2020. For some of them, it is doubled and even tripled. Recently, a pharmaceutical company announced a radical reorganization where managers will oversee up to 50 direct reports. Just two years ago, the average number of direct reports per manager was just 5; even at the largest firms, it peaked at 11.[10] The large number of direct reports can exacerbate a manager's arrogance, which can lead to decreased clarity for employees. In fact, a recent survey of global employees has shown that only 46% of employees know what is expected of them at work, only 30% strongly agree that someone at work encourages their development,[11] and 65% of employees feel underappreciated at work.[12] These feelings of fear and anxiety are only exacerbated when you are working for an arrogant boss. If this is the case for you, there are effective success strategies to consider.

Actions for Employees

Look for Ways to Strengthen Your Relationship with Your Manager

- Understand why your manager may exhibit arrogant behaviors and frame your communication style in ways that benefit your manager. Here are four ways to accomplish this:

    (1) Accentuate the positive: When meeting with your manager, acknowledge their perspective. As discussed above, knowing that an arrogant leader may have low self-esteem, acknowledge those areas where you agree or you think they have a good idea. For example, Megan's manager does not always act with arrogance, and when he has a good idea, she has decided to quickly acknowledge it and let him know she appreciates it.

    (2) Listen actively/Speak mindfully: Set your listening style so that your manager can do more of the talking and you do more of the listening. According to Adam Grant, "Silence is not always a sign of disengagement. It's usually better to think without speaking rather than to speak without thinking."[13]

    (3) Sit with it first/Take a moment: Pause before responding to a negative response from your manager. You want to make sure that you do not respond emotionally, but rather constructively.

    (4) Reframe alternatives: Rather than disagreeing with your manager, say things like "I have a suggestion that may help us in working with our customer success representatives."

Role Clarity

One large chain restaurant spent $10M and a quarter of a century in research to validate leadership ideas that worked.[14] The research concluded that the primary practice that was shown to elevate performance was *role clarity* – clearly defining roles and responsibilities. We have worked with many of our clients to design a process that ensures role clarity.

Megan and Terry have different ideas about what Megan is supposed to be doing. This is not surprising. Because arrogant leaders are often insecure, they are quick to criticize and hold back praise and recognition to feel better about themselves. Terry thrives on being vague because it gives him an out and puts more of the burden on Megan to interpret and deliver. For Megan it causes confusion around expectations. If you find yourself in Megan's situation, what can you do? The answer lies in following three strategies:[15]

- Clarify key job responsibilities
- Establish performance expectations
- Seek feedback

Clarify Key Job Responsibilities

Get a snapshot. The first thing to do is to get a "snapshot" of what your job consists of now. Most jobs can be broken down into about 5–10 key responsibilities, each including a cluster of critical job duties that you regularly accomplish. As a customer service supervisor, Megan has six key responsibilities:

1. Maintain customer relations
2. Maintain employee relations
3. Cooperate with other departments

4. Monitor computerized billing and credit system
5. Recruit and select customer success representatives
6. Administer company policies and procedures

Ask what is most important. Once the snapshot is taken, it's critical to think about the relative importance of the key responsibilities. After all, the importance of each responsibility has to do with the success of the organization, and can influence the amount of effort that you put in. A simple way to prioritize key responsibilities is to take 100 points and distribute them across the responsibilities. For instance, Megan's list might look like this:

1. Maintain customer relations (35 points)
2. Maintain employee relations (20 points)
3. Cooperate with other departments (10 points)
4. Monitor computerized billing and credit system (20 points)
5. Recruit and select customer success representatives (5 points)
6. Administer company policies and procedures (10 points)

This weighting clarifies the fact that Maintain customer relations and Maintain employee relations are the most important aspect of Megan's job, followed by Monitor computerized billing and credit system. The remaining three responsibilities are not as important to job success.

Involve your manager. It is vital that you share with your manager the key responsibilities of your job and their relative importance. A particularly good approach is for you to work on determining your key responsibilities and their weightings on your own and then show them to your manager. This creates a good forum for discussion and can lead to reconciling any differences and clarifying your job. If Megan had done this, and then shared it with Terry, it would have gone a long way to mutually align on her goals, which would reduce some of her anxiety and frustrations. At the very least, you have gone on record (and in writing) in sharing your perspective with your manager.

Establish Performance Expectations

Get agreement on what makes for success. Working with your manager as to your key responsibilities is only the initial step. You also need to agree on what constitutes success in those areas. Performance expectations are also about making your boss successful – which is even more relevant if you perceive your boss to be arrogant.

To do this, you and your manager should discuss *a minimum of five* performance expectations for each key responsibility. Performance expectations describe effective levels of performance for a given key responsibility. The expectations specify how your work is to be done and what you are to accomplish. They define the methods, behaviors, or actions you need to use in performing a particular key responsibility, and the outcomes that you are expected to achieve. Outcomes should be measurable (quantity, quality, or timeliness). One of Megan's key responsibilities – maintain employee relations – might include these four performance expectations:

1. Spend at least four hours per week working directly with the customer success representatives.
2. Invite customer success representatives' input before deciding on issues that will directly affect them.
3. Provide customer success representatives with new product information within two days of receiving it.

4. Clarify with each customer success representative what is expected regarding key responsibilities and performance expectations.

Ensure expectations are well-conceived. Good performance expectations have several characteristics:

1. they are under the employee's control
2. important to job success
3. challenging but not impossible
4. measurable or observable

Additionally, they should not be phrased in terms of personality traits. For instance, suppose initiative is important to success in your job, but initiative is a personality trait. The appropriate performance expectation is not the trait itself, but rather what you should do to show initiative; for example, "work longer hours without being asked when a deadline approaches" as opposed to "show initiative."

Involve your manager again. Just as you developed your key responsibilities by yourself and then discussed them with your manager, follow the same process with your performance expectations. Too often, employees bemoan the fact that they do not have a clear idea what their managers expect of them. On several occasions, Megan has vented her frustration to other supervisors saying, *"I often have no idea what Terry expects of me. I can only hope that we're on the same wavelength. I feel like he's too critical. At times, he seems resistant to my ideas or perspective."* If she had taken these two steps, first clarifying key job responsibilities and then establishing performance expectations, Megan would have shared her perspective and allowed her manager to respond. Unless these first two strategies are carefully undertaken, achieving success is like fumbling in the dark. Megan's role ambiguity only increases the probability of Terry exhibiting arrogant behaviors. How can Megan eliminate anxiety and achieve success when her path to success is never clarified?

We want to once again emphasize the importance of role clarity. Knowing that Terry has many additional direct reports than he has had in the past, Megan has carefully considered her key responsibilities and performance expectations. She also can monitor her own performance each month, by comparing her current level of performance with her performance expectations.

Seek Feedback

Sometimes if you ask your boss for advice, they will be more likely to think of future opportunities to improve rather than things you have done, which you can no longer change. Remember, your manager's arrogant behavior may be a cover for low self-esteem, and therefore, you want to avoid threatening behavior and ask for advice. Megan has recently had a serious customer complaint brought to her attention. She decided that it needed to be brought to Terry's attention, and she was very anxious about how he would react. To avoid another conflict, she decided that she would ask for his advice on how it should be handled and how these kinds of situations should be handled in the future. In this way, she was playing to his ego by asking for his advice and becoming more future oriented. This is a good tactic both for managing an arrogant boss AND for improving her performance – a win-win situation.

People who are working scared because of an arrogant boss need to actively seek out feedback from others, such as managers, co-workers, subordinates, and customers. Remember, our research has shown that employees who have more *arrogant* leaders rate their feedback environment less favorably, and they do not receive quality feedback that will allow them to make continual improvements in their own performance. It also helps you sustain high levels of job motivation and satisfaction. When you work with other people, you cannot ignore how they see your job performance. Any differences between your opinion and theirs should be discussed and resolved. Being successful on your key responsibilities and performance expectations not only helps you, but it helps your manager and the organization be more successful.

Here are three pointers to guide your feedback:

- **Focus on *your* key responsibilities and performance expectations.** Often, when your manager or a co-worker is dissatisfied with your performance, you will be compared unfavorably with other employees. It is disturbing and unhelpful; it tells you nothing about how you can improve your performance. To get quality feedback in this situation, you need to steer the conversation away from comparisons with others and toward your own key responsibilities and performance expectations.

- **Seek out continual feedback.** Don't wait until your end-of-the-year performance review to find out how you are doing. You certainly don't want feedback saved up and dumped on you all at one time. Instead, take it upon yourself to meet periodically with your manager to discuss how you are doing on each of your key responsibilities. You will recall from our story that Megan heard things that she had never heard before. This situation would never have occurred if Megan had sought regular feedback from Terry and others. Besides your manager, anyone inside or outside your organization who can observe your performance on one or more of your key responsibilities can supply you with meaningful feedback. This could include people from other departments that you work with regularly, co-workers, or even customers.

- **Seek feedback on behaviors or results.** People are often unaware of how to give feedback. You may receive reductive comments such as:
  - "You're too aggressive."
  - "You need to be more of a self-starter."
  - "You need to be more of a team player."

Comments like these are usually not personal attacks, but merely the person's lack of skill at describing the situation. Try to turn these comments into opportunities for improvement. To get to the heart of their feedback you could ask clarifying questions such as:

- "What have you seen me doing or not doing that makes you say that I am too aggressive?"
- "What is one thing – big or small – that I could do differently to be more of a self-starter or team player?"

By asking these questions, you encourage the person to be more specific and to discuss the behaviors or results that you are not accomplishing. Gathering developmental feedback through the three pointers above is what will help you achieve greater success and reduce your anxiety by only getting unhelpful feedback from your arrogant manager.

Succeeding Amidst Arrogant Leadership: The Blueprint for Employees

- Strengthen your position in the organization
- Understand why your manager may exhibit arrogant behaviors
- Focus on your key responsibilities and performance expectations/deliverables

- Document your contributions
- Seek feedback from those in your orbit
- Expand how you seek feedback

Actions for Leaders

We will discuss several strategies to help create a healthy and successful work culture. The model shown in Figure 2.1 shows the ripple effect of arrogant leadership, which creates a negative organizational culture. This negative culture in turn leads to decreased employee motivation and ultimately to decreased performance.

Below are some key actions that can lead to your success and along the way, keep your employees from working scared.

How Do You Know If You Are an Arrogant Leader?

Most leaders view themselves as confident, not arrogant. As such, arrogance is often a blind spot. While you may not have the opportunity to participate in a 360° feedback process as Terry did, below

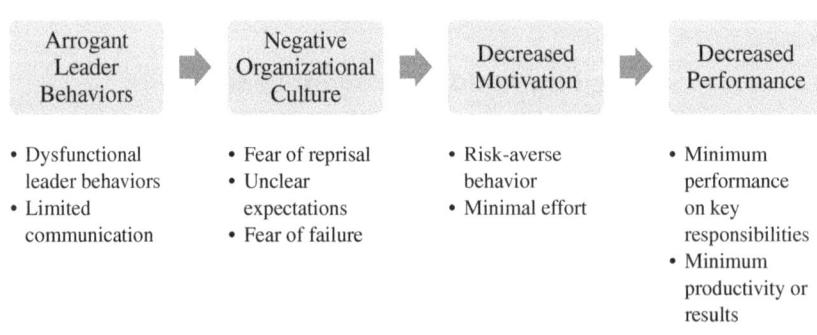

Figure 2.1 How Arrogant Leader Behaviors Affect Performance

are some questions that can help to ensure you are not perceived as arrogant.

Are you perceived as arrogant by your team?

On a scale of 1–5 (1 = never to 5 = always), please rate your answers to the following questions:

1. To what degree do you discredit others' ideas during meetings and consequently, make them look bad?
2. To what degree do you put your personal agenda above that of the organization?
3. To what degree do you reject constructive feedback?
4. To what degree do you take credit for success, but not blame for failures?
5. To what degree do you believe you know better than everyone else?
6. To what degree do you make decisions that impact others without asking for their input?

Now – ask your staff to anonymously complete the same questions concerning your leadership. Look for any items that are rated above "3." Total scores above 18 show you are leaning toward arrogance.[16]

Participate in a 360° Development Process

As mentioned above, all leaders at Terry's level and above have just recently participated in a 360° process to help each of them develop to become more effective leaders. Terry has had a highly successful career in the organization and has an excellent working relationship with his VP who has been very supportive of Terry through pay raises and promotions. Because of his success in the organization, Terry has always considered himself to be very confident, and he was sure that he would be rated well on the various leadership attributes by his staff, peers, and his boss. Terry was stunned when he received his feedback report. While his VP rated him high on the various leadership attributes, his direct reports and peers made it clear that he was seen as being arrogant. They were very unhappy with the work relationship that they had with Terry. There was a huge gap between how he perceived himself regarding arrogant behaviors versus how his direct reports and peers saw him. Knowing that his VP would see this information for the first time, not only were his direct reports working scared, including Megan, because of his arrogant behavior, but now, so was Terry! Below is a process that we have used with many of our clients to help them take advantage of the 360° process.

The process consists of four (4) main tools:

- **The 360° Leadership Development Instrument** is the questionnaire provided to multiple sources such as the individual leader, their manager, their direct reports, and their peers and others to provide insight into their level of effectiveness on numerous leadership attributes.
- **The 360° Feedback Report** provides the results of the self-ratings and ratings given to the individual leader by their manager, peers, and direct reports on the leadership attributes and individual items.
- **The 360° Development Workbook** will guide the individual through a series of activities to help them investigate and better understand the results of the Feedback Report.
- **The 360° Development Guide** will provide many recommended behavioral strategies, activities, and readings for developing on specific Leadership Attributes.

As a result of the above process, Terry has made a commitment to his VP that he would establish better working relationships with his direct reports and peers. He also committed to conducting another 360° survey a year from now and pledged to show significant improvements. Therefore, Terry needs to ask himself what he can do when faced with the need for change. What are the consequences of not changing, and how can changing make him more successful in his career? Individuals are more likely to change in response to feedback when the organization makes employees accountable for change. Terry's boss made it markedly clear that he expects to see meaningful change with regard to his arrogant behavior over the next year.

Communicate Your Willingness to Change and Listen

To keep your employees from working scared and to help ensure you are not being perceived as arrogant, be transparent in your communications with your staff. For example, Terry let his direct reports know that he took the feedback about his arrogance seriously. He committed to change and would like to participate in the 360° feedback survey next year with the goal that his direct reports will see the change in his behavior.

To ensure that you are not perceived as arrogant, be willing to listen to opposing viewpoints. Focus on understanding what the individual is saying rather than trying to formulate what your response will be. In this way, you avoid interrupting until the individual has finished making their points. Remember, you do not always have to be the smartest person in the room; others may have good points.

When making decisions that impact others, listen to their input. Listen to your staff to understand how you can help them maximize their performance. Research has shown that when employees feel heard, their engagement rises and their performance improves, delivering benefits to their companies.[17] Be sure to always remember to show empathy by making space for others to feel heard, not filling the silence with your own experiences.[18]

It is a good idea to recognize contributions publicly, check in informally, and model calm under pressure.[19] Sometimes you simply need to admit a mistake, apologize, and move on. By admitting mistakes, you are showing vulnerability, and it encourages others to be honest as well. In some cases, it helps to publicly acknowledge your errors and share lessons learned.[20]

All these behaviors can communicate your willingness to change and listen and go a long way to building trust and keeping your employees from working scared!

Give Effective Feedback

As stated earlier in the chapter, our consulting experience and our research shows that when a leader is perceived as arrogant, the feedback environment or culture is perceived as being less favorable by employees. Terry committed to sitting down with Megan and with each of his other direct reports to clarify key responsibilities and performance expectations. This will allow for the feedback that he gives to be more productive and supportive of their development efforts. He committed to tying his feedback, both positive and negative, back to their key responsibilities and performance expectations. Very few employees can maintain high levels of motivation without effective feedback.

To ensure that the feedback you give to an employee is appropriate, positive or negative, ask yourself the following[21]:

- **Does the feedback fit the employee?**
  - Will it be meaningful enough to help the employee improve?

- Is the feedback appropriate, in the sense that the employee feels he or she deserves it?
- Is the feedback something the employee values?
- **Is the focus of the feedback specific enough?**
  - Is it directly related to employee job performance?
  - What did the employee specifically do that deserves feedback?
  - How does it help the employee, the department, and the organization?
- **Is the feedback timely?**
  - Is it given soon after the behavior occurs? The closer to the behavior the feedback occurs, the more impact it will have on future performance. The more the feedback fits the person involved, focuses on specific job performance, and occurs soon enough after the behavior, the greater the effect on your employee's performance.

**Succeeding Amidst Arrogant Leadership:
The Blueprint for Leaders**

- Become an enlightened leader through feedback
- Create a culture of feedback through a 360° process
- Communicate your willingness to change
- Collaborate for role clarity
- Ensure that the feedback you give to employees is appropriate

Workplace Arrogance Scale[22]

1 (Strongly Disagree) to 5 (Strongly Agree)

This individual:

1. Believes that they know better than everyone else in any given situation.
2. Makes decisions that impact others without listening to their input.
3. Uses nonverbal behaviors like glaring or staring to make people uncomfortable.
4. Criticizes others.
5. Belittles their employees publicly.
6. Asserts authority in situations when they don't have the required information.
7. Discredits others' ideas during meetings and often makes those individuals look bad.
8. Shoots down other people's ideas in public.
9. Exhibits different behaviors with subordinates than with supervisors.
10. Makes unrealistic time demands on others.
11. Does not find it necessary to explain their decisions to others.
12. Takes him/herself too seriously.
13. *Willing to listen to others' opinions, ideas, or perspectives.
14. *Welcomes constructive feedback.
15. *Takes responsibility for his/her own mistakes.

16. *Never criticizes other employees in a threatening manner.
17. *Realizes that it does not always have to be "his/her way or the highway."
18. *Avoids getting angry when their ideas are criticized.
19. *Gives others credit for their ideas.
20. *Is considerate of others' workloads.
21. *Is willing to take credit for success as well as blame for failure.
22. *Does not mind doing menial tasks.
23. *Can get others to pay attention without getting emotionally "heated up."
24. *Promises to address subordinates' complaints with every intention of working to resolve them.
25. *Does not see him/herself as being too important for some tasks.
26. *Puts organizational objectives before his/her personal agenda.

*These items are reverse scored.

Workplace Arrogance

This dimension refers to an individual's expression of arrogance in the workplace. A leader high on this dimension is likely not trusted by employees. They do not value the advice and feedback from others and do not handle criticism well. A leader low on this dimension tends to be more respected by colleagues, and listens to others' ideas, feedback, and criticism. A leader who displays arrogance may have employees that dislike him or her. Leaders that are *low* on the dimension of arrogance demonstrate the following behaviors:

1. Puts organizational goals before personal goals
2. Takes credit for failures as well as successes
3. Willing to listen to others' thoughts, ideas, and concerns
4. Embraces feedback from others
5. Respects others' ideas/opinions
6. Does not get angry or defensive about negative feedback
7. Willing to own up to mistakes
8. Gives credit where credit is due
9. Believes that coaching and training can be beneficial and worthwhile
10. Willing to learn from others
11. Willing to work with others to settle disagreements
12. Listens to others' concerns
13. Realizes there is more than one way to solve a problem
14. Willing to ask for help from others
15. Is considerate of others' workloads

Chapter 3

Amplifying Your Voice in a Team Culture

How to Open Up Dialogue Even When It Feels Risky

Have you ever felt reluctant to speak up or hesitated to ask a question in a team meeting? Have you held back a fresh idea or unique perspective, worrying it wouldn't be accepted? Or maybe you went along with the majority opinion because it felt uncomfortable to disagree? You're not alone. Most of us can relate to these moments. At one point or another, we've chosen silence over speaking up, often driven by fear.

We are working scared – in silence.

Now imagine the cost of those quiet moments in a team: the good ideas that go unspoken, the thought-provoking questions that never get asked, the unsaid insights that could have shifted a decision or changed the course of work. In an environment of accelerating change and daily pressure to perform, we need fresh thinking now more than ever. The most effective employees find ways to lend their voice – not only to contribute to team success, but to shape their own. And the most effective leaders actively foster an environment where voice is encouraged and valued.

What stops us? It's easy to assume that speaking up at work is simple – just share an idea, raise a concern, or offer feedback. But in practice, many of us hesitate at the most critical moments. Even the team members with valuable insights often stay quiet during meetings, downplay their contributions, or withhold dissenting views. And it's not because they have nothing to say. It's because the perceived risks outweigh the perceived reward.

And the risk is real. "Organizational silence" is a term that describes a systemic pattern where employees fear negative repercussions for speaking up.[1] They think if they speak up, they might be perceived as difficult or, worse yet, they may experience repercussions that impede their career progression. People often remain silent not due to a lack of ideas, but because they worry how their comments might be received, and they fear harming their image or their standing in the group.[2] In environments shaped by power dynamics, strong personalities, or unspoken norms, silence becomes the safer – and far more common – response.

In our work, we regularly hear stories of people choosing to stay silent even if the potential consequences of speaking up are modest. It's often hard to find your voice in a team setting. We want to help you ease the fear so that you can speak up and encourage your team members to do the same. We want to increase the reward of speaking and reduce the risk.

Let's Look at Some Facts

- Most of us will be new to teams many times in our careers. The average worker born between 1957 and 1964 has more than 12 jobs over the course of their career.[3] Job switching is increasing. Newer entrants into the workforce can expect even more career changes. Each change requires a new employee to find a voice in a new team.
- Psychological safety is the belief that you can speak up with ideas, questions, concerns, or mistakes without fear of repercussions.[4] It is a prerequisite for open communication.

- In a recent McKinsey study, 89% of respondents said they believe that psychological safety in the workplace is essential to speaking up.[5] When psychological safety is low, retention decreases – 12% of employees in teams with low psychological safety are likely to quit within a year, compared with just 3% in high-psychological-safety environments.[6]
- Employee silence is frequently driven by fear, not disinterest. In fact, many organizational cultures reinforce the notion that speaking up is "rocking the boat."[7]

Merritt's Story

Merritt is a mid-level manager at a nationwide accounting firm. He has worked successfully as an auditor for 12 years and recently transferred within the company to a high-performing but close-knit, well-established team. Merritt's new manager, Elisabeth, recruited him based on his strong past performance. Merritt was excited about the new opportunity to apply his skills and experience in a new setting with lots of developmental opportunities. He respected Elisabeth and was eager to make a strong impression.

Elisabeth is known as an inspiring but demanding leader. She sets a high bar for herself and her direct reports. She views herself as someone who encourages divergent voices. This is something that Merritt especially appreciated. In his first weeks on the job, Merritt attended several team meetings that included 12 colleagues. Half were typically on-site in the office, with the other half dialing in from home offices across the country.

Merritt felt a bit overwhelmed by the dynamics in the meetings. They were fast-paced and action-oriented. Merritt noticed

(continued)

(continued)

that ideas flowed, but mostly from the same handful of voices in the room. Those voices usually reinforced time-tested ways of doing things. Meanwhile, the team members who joined virtually were largely silent. While Merritt knew he was hired to bring in new ideas, each time he considered speaking up, he hesitated. "They already have a rhythm," he thought. *"It is too hard to disrupt the flow with my idea."*

As the weeks passed, Merritt found himself holding back his comments and contributions. He gave in to the fear that speaking up might be misinterpreted or seen as an unwelcome outsider's perspective. One evening, he described the situation to his wife. He told her he planned to play it safe, at least until he better understood the team dynamics. His wife tried to convince him otherwise. *"Elisabeth recruited you for your talents, not to be passive and silent,"* she said. Then she said something that shifted his thinking: *"You say that being silent is playing it safe. Maybe being silent is even more dangerous than speaking up."* In those early weeks, Merritt realized he was making a first impression. Maybe silence wasn't the impression he wanted to give. Being new to the team, he had a unique opportunity to ask questions and offer fresh observations – and to be seen as a valuable contributor, not a passive bystander. Though he knew she was right, he was unsure what to do next.

Actions for Employees

Speaking up often feels risky – especially in a new team setting. What holds us back in these types of situations is the fear of being wrong, the worry about how others might react, and the uncertainty about possible consequences. In these moments, fear overrides the best of intentions. People are literally scared into silence.

In this section, we offer techniques that can help mitigate some of these effects. The suggestions we offer can help shift the balance toward speaking and enable you to incrementally gain voice even in the most challenging environments. They are techniques that you can practice over time, gradually expanding your capacity to speak up.

Observe and Listen

While we encourage you to speak, it is important to do so thoughtfully. Therefore, we recommend that, before speaking, take some time to observe and listen; we call this the "Eyes and Ears First" approach. This is a chance to collect data. Once you've collected a few observations, be prepared to share them. Even when you don't have much to say, you can still offer a contribution based on what you have seen and heard. This technique is best when it is a combination of an observation with a question, rather than a declarative statement. Frame the contribution with the following simple structure:

> *"I have noticed . . ., and what I'm wondering is . . ."*

In working with Merritt, we helped him apply this approach in his team meetings. He paused to notice something nobody else saw, a pattern that seemed to be holding the team back. Rather than forcing his way into the fast-paced dynamic, he tried a different, gentler approach. He started by observing the room. He took note of who spoke most, who stayed silent, what themes emerged, and what topics never got addressed. He noticed that in a few conversations, the team circled back to the same planning dilemma: how to allocate limited staff across several high-priority clients during tax season. The people in the room were talking over each other, but the issue was never actually resolved.

At the next meeting, Merritt didn't launch into a critique but shared an observation. He simply said, "I've noticed this topic has come up a few times, and what I'm wondering, is there a different way we could approach it?" It was a simple question, based on an observation, and – importantly – free of judgment. It turns out that his observation served as a gentle nudge that helped the team change course. His outside perspective combined with a simple, confident question helped break the routine in a constructive way. The team began to explore a lingering challenge in a new way that they had previously ignored.

What Merritt did was not dramatic. He took his time to observe, collecting "data" before lending his voice. He entered the conversation through curiosity rather than as a critique based on what he saw and heard, not any special expertise. And Elisabeth took notice. She realized that someone new to the team was best positioned to make such an observation, and she expressed genuine gratitude for Merritt's fresh perspective.

You can use the Eyes and Ears First approach to bring your voice into any team setting by:

1. taking the time to watch and listen,
2. offering an observation, and then
3. asking a simple question.

Reframe What Speaking Up Means

Often, we suppress a contribution because we think our message will not be well received. We often hear from our clients, both employees and leaders, that people speak up only when they have something negative to say, such as a complaint or a problem. But what if we wanted to say something positive? In such cases, it would be much easier to speak. And the message would more likely be well received. Distinguish between potentially threatening messages from those that can be more easily shared. There is a wide array of messages that can raise your voice in a team through a welcome contribution. In fact, there are often far more positive messages left unsaid than complaints. In Figure 3.1, the left side of the figure represents how people often view speaking up – as mostly negative. But the right side reframes it, showing how negative messages are only a small part of the larger pie of possible contributions. Practice with easier messages, such as observations, questions, suggestions, and encouragement. It will then be easier to convey more difficult messages – such as asking for help, sharing a critique, voicing disagreement – when such situations inevitably arise.

When Merritt offered his observation, Elisabeth and the rest of the team appreciated the comment because it came across as constructive and thoughtful. He pointed out that the topic of resource planning had surfaced several times but remained unresolved. No one could dispute the accuracy of what he noticed. Rather than criticizing the team or

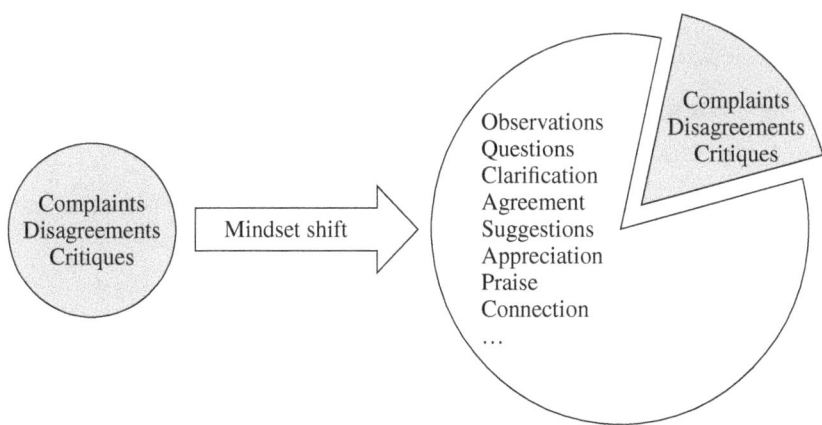

Figure 3.1 Mindset Shift to Expand the Space for Speaking Up

positioning himself as the expert, Merritt posed a question that invited others to explore the issue together. His tone was factual, curious, and forward-looking making it possible for his voice to be heard – and easy for others to receive his message. Remember that Merritt did not need extensive knowledge or expertise to make this contribution. He simply had to pay attention. This kind of low-risk contribution is a powerful way to make your voice heard in a team, without fear.

Use the 5W Framework

When you're preparing to speak up – particularly if the message feels sensitive, important, uncertain, or high-stakes – take a moment to reflect and be intentional about the message. Use our 5W Framework: Why, What, Who, When, and Where. The following prompts can help you to prepare:

1. **Why** do I feel this message is important?
2. **What** exactly do I want to say? What's the best way to say it?
3. **Who** needs to hear this (e.g., just my manager or the whole team)? Would it help to test my message with a trusted colleague first?
4. **When** is the best occasion to say it (e.g., is now the right time or should I wait?)
5. **Where** should this message be shared (e.g., in a formal meeting, a casual check-in, or a written follow-up)?

Thinking through the answers to each of these questions can help you clarify your intent, choose the right audience, and increase the chance your message will land well.

Not every contribution needs this level of preparation. But if you find yourself holding back, then planning the 5Ws of your message will make it easier to gain your voice by helping you think through all the essential elements of your message. And once you've started gaining your voice through planning, you will become more comfortable offering unplanned and unprompted contributions more often.

Build Your Voice in Trusted Circles

It is true that speaking up in some situations will feel riskier than others, and a risky environment will inevitably inhibit our voice. A useful technique is to begin with trusted peers where you can test out ideas and messages. As your confidence grows, challenge yourself to push beyond that comfort zone. Offer bolder contributions or speak up in riskier settings. This progression is key to strengthening your capacity to use your voice. Finding your voice is an ongoing process – even for a seasoned professional.

Merritt, for instance, considered himself a confident, capable, and experienced accountant who was normally comfortable speaking up. But something about the dynamics in his new team silenced him in the first few meetings. So, he applied this technique. He decided to reach out to a former colleague. Specifically, he contacted Sebastian, with whom he'd worked in his prior role in the company. Sebastian was known for challenging people's thinking. Merritt used their trusted relationship to test his message. He shared the observations he had of his new team's meetings, and he worked with Sebastian to fine-tune the question he would pose. Merritt felt ready. Had he needed more preparation, he could have expanded his trusted circle. For example, he could discuss his idea with friendly members of his new team, or he could have had a conversation with Elisabeth. These are all ways Merritt could overcome his hesitation and find his voice in the team.

> **Finding Your Voice in a Team Culture:
> The Blueprint for Employees**
>
> - Observe and listen ("Eyes and Ears First") to collect data
> - Build your confident voice, step-by-step, by starting with easier messages
> - Use the 5W Framework to prepare for high-stakes messages
> - Test your messages with safe peers to build your confidence
> - Frame your comments to open up the dialogue
> - Amplify your voice through regular practice – and help others find their voice

Actions for Leaders

As we emphasize throughout this book, you as a leader play the primary role in setting the tone for the culture in your team. No high performing team can survive the rigors of business without good ideas bubbling to the surface. And no great team can have perpetually silent members. Leaders often overestimate how easy it is to speak up. When we conduct 360° assessments, we often discover an inconsistency: team leaders think they encourage contribution while many of their own team members describe being hesitant to speak up. Fear overwhelms them and valuable contributions remain unspoken. It is vital to create an environment where it is safe to speak. This does not mean a free-for-all. There are times when decisions will be made without full team support or when an idea will be overruled. But fear of speaking cripples a team over the long term. You as a leader need to create conditions where fear is minimized.

Change the Risk–Reward Calculus

So long as your employees perceive the risk of speaking as being greater than the reward, they will remain silent. Your response makes all the difference. When a poor suggestion gets punished and a useful one is met with indifference, why would anyone risk speaking up? On the other hand, if an infeasible idea gets a gentle correction and an innovative idea is met with high praise, your team members will take note and more freely share ideas. The risk–reward calculus is demonstrated with two simple scenarios:

Scenario 1: Risk > Reward = Employees Stay Silent

When the perceived risk of speaking up is greater than the potential reward, employees are *less likely* to speak up. For example, imagine an employee suggesting a change to an established process during a meeting. The idea is quickly dismissed, and the employee is later excluded from a project. Others in the room take note of that response. The message is clear: speaking up could lead to disapproval or negative consequences. As a result, even valid contributions go unspoken, and psychological safety erodes over time.

Scenario 2: Risk < Reward = Employees Speak up

When the potential reward is greater than the perceived risk, employees are *more likely* to contribute. Imagine an employee proposes a new idea that ultimately isn't feasible. Rather than shutting it down, the manager explains why it won't work, thanks the employee for thinking creatively, and encourages more suggestions. This kind of respectful, appreciative response makes others feel safe to contribute and lowers the risk. The more leaders reinforce these positive moments, the more likely employees will speak up again.

As a leader, you are constantly shaping the implicit risk–reward calculus of communication. Every comment you acknowledge, appreciate, dismiss, or ignore sends a signal about what's safe to say and what isn't. To encourage voice in your team, ensure your reaction sends the message that thoughtful contributions are welcomed, respected, and rewarded.

Invite All the Voices – Early and Often

Set the expectation for engagement by building time into every meeting agenda for team members to share their voice. Our experience shows that when you hear from everyone *early* in a meeting, you are much more likely to encourage dynamic contributions *throughout* the meeting. We worked with a leader who typically devoted the last ten minutes of a weekly virtual meeting to discussion, only to find lackluster participation. Most participants had their cameras off and stayed on mute; he suspected most were multitasking. The disengagement frustrated him. So, he redesigned his agenda, devoting the first five minutes to a "check-in" during which he collected themes and open questions from each participant. By hearing every voice right from the start, he lowered the barrier to speaking for the remainder of the meeting. Engagement skyrocketed as a result.

Don't let your meetings become packed with presentations and monotonous status updates. If you do, the likely result will be one person speaking after another with little real interaction. If there's no interaction, why have a meeting at all? If a meeting is just to convey information, you might be better off just sending a document for everyone to read and thereby save the time spent meeting. The whole point of getting together is, in fact, to engage with one another. As a leader, you typically have influence over an agenda. Use that power to make sure there's space for interaction in every meeting and with each agenda item.

In our experience, how you ask for input significantly affects the level of participation. Consider the difference in tone among these three ways of inviting input after a presentation:

(1) Are there any questions?

(2) What questions are there?

(3) Let's have some questions. I'd love to hear everyone's thoughts.

The first approach generates a high barrier to feedback. It's phrased in a way that makes it easy for people to stay silent, especially if they're unsure whether their question will be seen as smart, relevant, or welcome. People often interpret this question as rhetorical, especially when it comes at the end of a presentation. It can feel like the speaker is signaling the session is over rather than genuinely inviting input. Team members may worry that asking a question might suggest they missed something obvious, slow things down, or be seen as challenging the presenter. As a result, only the most outspoken or confident participants will respond.

The second approach lowers the barrier by assuming that questions exist, sending the message that questions are expected and encouraged. It takes the pressure off participants to justify why they're speaking and frames questions as a natural part of engagement rather than as a disruption. This phrasing invites interaction without putting anyone on the spot, making it more comfortable for less vocal team members to participate.

The third approach offers a warm and inclusive invitation to participate. It signals that you are genuinely interested in hearing participant voices, not just the usual ones. The barrier is very low, especially for quieter team members who may need extra encouragement. The language humanizes the interaction and normalizes everyone's contribution.

One of our clients, a plant manager, offers a good example of this practice in action. He regularly held town hall meetings with the large staff at his manufacturing site. His main goal was to share information, but he also hoped the meetings would spark genuine interaction with the larger team. He delivered performance updates, shared company news, and acknowledged birthdays and work anniversaries. At the end, he would ask, "Are there any questions?" Nobody ever responded. On one occasion, in a lighthearted moment of desperation at the end a presentation, he smiled and said, "somebody please ask me a question." People chuckled, and, to his delight, several hands went up. In that instance, he lowered the barrier to input. And the questions he got were insightful and important. That experience taught him an important lesson: silence usually isn't a sign of disinterest – it's a sign of fear. By actively inviting input, leaders reduce fear and increase the chances of surfacing valuable contributions that would otherwise remain hidden.

Be Clear, Be Consistent

Leaders often say they want open dialogue, but their behavior tells a different story. When team members share dissenting views or ask tough questions, leaders may react with visible frustration – especially if that input slows momentum or challenges a planned course of action. Over time, these mixed signals erode trust, increase fear, and make employees more hesitant to contribute.

To cultivate a genuine culture of voice, you need to align your words with actions. That means welcoming input even when it may be inconvenient. It also means being clear and transparent when an extended discussion is not possible because a decision needs to be made quickly. There will be moments when you need to move on – the meeting is ending, a deadline looms, or the team has enough information to proceed. When you need to intervene to end a discussion, don't let these moments undermine the culture of contribution you've worked hard to build. Instead, be clear and respectful. Say something like, "We'll need to end the debate and move forward for now, but I still want to hear your perspectives. I'll follow-up with you individually." Communicating the "why" behind limiting discussion reinforces trust and signals that open contribution remains your team's core value – even when time is tight and the pressure to perform is intense.

Appreciate the Effort

Show your appreciation for the contributions to reinforce the behavior and encourage voice in your team. This increases the reward for speaking. By acknowledging contributions, even briefly, you reinforce the behavior and signal that you notice and value speaking up. It's the effort to participate – not just the brilliance of the idea – that deserves appreciation. To do this, we recommend a simple phrase such as "that's a helpful observation" or "I appreciate you raising that," which can go a long way in building trust. We stress that appreciation does not have to mean your agreement, but it should convey respect for the effort it took to share an idea, especially when it carries risk. Over time, consistent acknowledgment helps normalize voice as a team norm, not a rare act of courage or something for the most outspoken team members.

Elisabeth modeled this behavior effectively. When Merritt shared his observation, she responded with genuine appreciation for Merritt's effort to share his perspective. And she did so in front of the team. Her reaction not only helped Merritt find voice but also encouraged the same thing from others in the team. Remember that every response to a comment is an opportunity to strengthen your team's culture and reinforce constructure behaviors.

Set and Reinforce Interaction Principles

Your team may have clear rules for what needs to be done and how – but have you ever discussed *how* to interact? Co-creating team norms builds buy-in for interaction principles and it clarifies expectations for collaboration. Try exploring questions such as:

- How can we interact to bring out the best in each other?
- How do we ensure each person has a chance to contribute?
- What can help us stick to the principles we set?

Based on our work with teams, here are some helpful examples of interaction principles:

- **Each voice matters.** We give everyone space to contribute and listen actively – not just wait for our turn to speak.
- **Don't interrupt.** We let others fully express their ideas before responding. We take turns.
- **"Yes, and . . .".** We try to build on each other's ideas. We avoid "No, but . . ." responses that can shut down conversation.

Once you have your team's interaction principles, make sure to reinforce them. If you notice that some people dominate conversations while others fall silent, return to the principles you set together. Gently remind your team what they agreed to. Anybody on the team can reinforce the principles; but as the team leader, your influence carries extra weight.

Provide Development Opportunities

Speaking up is a skill that can be learned and developed. Leaders likely underestimate how hard it is to speak. In fact, for leaders who have risen in an organization by sharing their voice, it is easy to forget how intimidating it can be for some to speak – especially for new team members. Demonstrate your commitment to building voice by creating opportunities for growth. This might include formal activities such as giving a presentation, conducting a workshop, or attending an executive communication class. Informal opportunities could include coaching, assigning someone a speaking role in a team meeting, or simply encouraging low-stakes opportunities to contribute like asking for a quick summary of a group discussion or sharing a personal perspective during a team debrief. You can even introduce some of the tools from this book – like the Eyes and Ears First – to help team members practice, thereby building their confidence and presence over time.

All the techniques mentioned will enhance your team's comfort in speaking up. Your employees will feel safe to speak without fear of negative consequences. This contributes to innovation, resilience, commitment, and long-term team performance.

**Finding Your Voice in a Team Culture:
The Blueprint for Leaders**

- Change the risk–reward calculus to make the risk of speaking up worthwhile
- Invite all the voices – early and often – to encourage contribution
- Manage your reaction
- Set and follow your team's "interaction principles"
- Provide development opportunities

Chapter 4

Thriving in a Hybrid Team

From the Office to Remote to Somewhere In-Between

Millions of global workers have gone from working fully on site, to working exclusively remote, and then going to a hybrid model. It should not be surprising that workers are having to adapt to this rapid organizational change and are working scared. Let's start by looking at some facts.

Let's Look at Some Facts

In 2025, just 21% of US employees with remote-capable jobs were fully on-site, compared with 52% working hybrid and 27% working exclusively remote. And 60% of remote-capable workers now say hybrid is their preferred way to work. Remote-capable, on-site employees have experienced the largest drop in engagement since 2020. These individuals have a job that could be performed with remote flexibility, but instead, they are required to work on-site every workday.[1] The same survey showed that according to hybrid employees they found the following benefits:

- Improved work-life balance – 76%
- Most efficient use of time throughout the day/week – 64%

- Less burnout or fatigue at work – 61%
- More freedom to choose when or where to work – 57%
- Higher productivity – 52%

Despite the benefits discussed above from the employee perspective, many organizations prefer their employees to return to work for a variety of perceived reasons. They cite increased productivity and financial performance, better collaboration among the employees, a more effective culture, and having more control. This creates tension that can have employees working scared in a hybrid model.

Below are three hybrid work trends that organizations need to pay attention to[2]:

1. Organizations that embrace a hybrid model will have greater successful talent recruitment than those organizations that have harsh return-to-office (RTO) requirements.
2. Enlightened organizations will shift toward measuring employee outcomes and not time in office.
3. Organizations will need to have flexible hybrid policies. Attempting to have rigid RTO policies such as four days in office will have significant issues for teams that are spread across locations. These kinds of policies can lead to significant employee departures.

In this chapter, we will discuss effective strategies that both employees and leaders can implement to be more successful in a hybrid environment. Of particular emphasis, we will show how employees and leaders can work together to maximize their individual as well as their team's performance.

Kendall's Story

Kendall works in customer support for a large technology company in Denver. Prior to the global pandemic, she really enjoyed working in the office. Ryan, her director, was a good leader who trusted the team and was there if she needed him. If she had a question, she could easily walk into his office and have it answered. In addition, Kendall really liked the team she worked with – hey were friendly and outgoing, and they had a good time working together in the office. They were collaborative and always there for each other whether to offer help or solve problems.

Then the global pandemic forced office closures, and the entire staff of the company's large office building had to work remotely. As a result, the company gave up approximately 50% of its office space to save on unnecessary expenses. Kendall adapted quickly to remote working. She liked managing her own time, taking care of personal matters between meetings, and avoiding a long commute. However, she felt disconnected. Ryan's effective leadership style, when they were all in the office, did not translate as well to a remote work environment. The collaboration and direction that she always appreciated from him was not as effective or helpful when working remotely. She was also not sure Ryan knew everything she was working on or the progress she was making.

Last month, Ryan told the team that the company announced a new "return-to-office" policy that required all employees to be in the office 2–3 days a week. Kendall was initially excited by this hybrid approach. She thought she could get the best of both worlds – a renewed sense of team spirit from office days with the freedom she cherished when working from home.

(continued)

(continued)

Now, one month into the new policy, she is disappointed. Instead of getting the upside of a home and office environment, neither one fully meets her expectations. And Kendall was not the only one who felt this way. Because of the move from remote to hybrid work, a couple of her colleagues have left the company and, as a result, the team has several new members. Now, in the hybrid environment, she is frustrated by a few important things.

First, Kendall feels she has lost the ability to use her time most efficiently and has also lost the flexibility to handle day care challenges for her children. Second, when the company reduced office space, they created an open office design. The company thought this would save on facility costs and promote collaboration. But the office is now very noisy, and Kendall finds it hard to concentrate. Also, since most people come to the office mid-week, it's overcrowded on those days.

One of the things she was excited about, with the return-to-office policy, was that she thought she could pop over to a colleague's desk to ask questions or share best practices. However, when she now goes into the office, she feels that communication with other employees has not improved because she never knows who is in the office on any given day. Kendall's feeling of unpredictability surrounding the hybrid RTO policy has her worried, not just about a potential drop in her productivity, but her work-life balance as well. She fears she is giving up the freedom of working remotely while not seeing the benefits of returning to the office. Feeling unsettled has caused Kendall to work scared.

Actions for Employees

In a hybrid work arrangement, employees must pay extra attention to how they complete their work, interact with managers and peers, and build team relationships. Things we take for granted in the office – like meeting informally with colleagues – or in a purely remote arrangement – like managing your own time – become more complex in a hybrid environment. Therefore, we offer actions to help you reduce the fear that comes from this uncertainty.

Track and Share

It's imperative to effectively track your work, record any questions you have, and create an organized agenda for your 1:1 meetings with your manager. Discuss what progress you have made toward your goals since your last meeting. For example, you can provide more visibility that your manager may not have known about. The more you can advocate for yourself, the more likely you are to excel in your role or be considered for advancement to the next one.

Ask for Advice

If you need support and you feel like you are left on your own, always ask your manager for advice and share your feelings. We worked with Kendall to coach her in meeting with Ryan. In their one-on-one meetings, Kendall asked Ryan for advice about how they could enhance communication among the team members. Kendall told Ryan that while she wanted to enhance communication, she never knew who was going to be in the office on any given day. Her feelings were exacerbated by the fact that they had two new team members. Ryan agreed that this was an issue, and that he would think about having one or two anchor days where everyone would be required to be in the office each week. Ryan promised he would then get back to her. He was receptive and Kendall was glad she brought the issue up by asking for his advice.

Use Your Office Time

Use your in-office days to meet with your manager and have more informal conversations than you would when you were working remotely. When possible, spend time with your peers and co-workers to build more effective relationships. Kendall used this time to get to know her new team members. Have fun together to build relationships – go to lunch or arrange a team event after work to get to know one another better. These things will help you build more trust with your colleagues. Focus on developing meaningful relationships with team members during your time together.

Enhance Cross-Functional Relationships

During the global pandemic, exclusive remote work coupled with high turnover (often referred to as the great resignation) resulted in fewer and weaker peer and cross-functional relationships. Relationships became more transactional, resulting in a lower commitment to colleagues and the broader organization. We discussed with Kendall that we have found that during this time, people would show up for calls, and as soon as the call ended, they went about their priorities without a sense of ownership or commitment to the host's priorities (just to their own individual tasks and responsibilities). This is particularly problematic for heavy cross-functional tasks. As we transition to hybrid work, it's critical to focus on re-establishing meaningful relationships. The deterioration of relationships has resulted in cross-functional teams reducing their sense of ownership. We stressed to Kendall that by developing meaningful relationships, people will feel more accountable to each other and increase their commitment to delivering a common goal together. For example, when Kendall was in the office, she made a point of meeting for coffee with an individual member of a cross-functional team that she was on. She felt that by building a stronger personal relationship with these team members, they were more motivated, and they accomplished more on the cross-functional projects they were working on.

Promote Open Communication Using "5 Tips"

While the following communications tips can be applied to any team, they are particularly critical when working on a hybrid team.

Convey Equality and Mutual Respect

It's very unlikely that everybody on your team possesses the same level of talent, experience, ability, power, or status. In fact, given that Kendall has new team members, she might be one of the more talented or powerful members of her team. If so, she must be especially careful about her tone. If she conveys superiority, she will stifle openness.

Communicate Mindfully

Kendall must be careful not to say things like the following:

- "I've been around here long enough to know that it won't work."
- "If you had listened to what I told you before, we wouldn't be having all these problems."
- "After you've been here as long as I have, you'll understand what I mean."

What Kendall needs to do is to treat team members in a way that clearly communicates:

- "I respect your ideas."
- "I'm listening, even though I see things differently."
- "I value your opinion."
- "We're all in this together."

Provide Specific Behaviors

Using the terms "always" or "never" when discussing a team member's job performance can be a major putdown. Telling people that they are "always late for team meetings" or "never willing to pitch in" will inevitably make them angry and defensive. You'll do much better simply saying: "Jane, I've noticed that sometimes you've been showing up late for team meetings" or "Alex, how about giving us a hand?" Stay far away from sweeping statements, even if they are accurate.

Focus on the Issue

When disagreeing with another team member, focus on the issue, not the person. Personal attacks – such as "you're dead wrong," "you don't know what you're talking about," "you've missed the point," "you're being foolish," "you're naïve, if you can believe that," and "if you'd listen better, you'd understand what I mean" – are destructive because they belittle the other person's self-esteem. Instead, you need to keep your disagreements centered on the issue. Use statements such as "here's where I think we disagree," "as I see it," and "here's what I think the main point is."

Stay Away from Gotcha! Statements

The game of "I gotcha" is deadly in a team environment. When team members are told things such as "I told you so" and "See, I was right all along," it isn't long before they stop contributing altogether. These kinds of put-downs, while never helpful, should always be avoided.

Learn to Listen

Listening goes beyond merely hearing. It also involves being open-minded and willing to seriously consider other viewpoints. Effective team players show more interest in the success of their team than in being proven "right." They're willing to listen to opposing viewpoints to find the ideas that are in the best interest of their team.

Show Empathy

Team members stop communicating with others on their team who act as though their feelings and welfare are not important. The opposite of this attitude is empathy. What can Kendall say to show her fellow team members that she shares their concerns? Here are a few suggestions we gave to Kendall:

- "I understand how you feel."
- "I'd feel the same way if I were in your position."
- "What can I do to help you out?"

Segment Your Time to Optimize Results

As you allocate time, it's appropriate to segment your efforts by your work environment. For many, deep work is better when working from home. When we discussed the importance of segmenting work with Kendall, she realized that when she had to work on a project and really needed to concentrate, she was better off working from home. On the other hand, she told us that developing relationships, cross-functional alignment efforts, brainstorming activities, group work sessions, etc. are all better for the in-office work environment. Kendall ultimately felt that allocating her time in accordance with the work environment positively impacts her efficiency and effectiveness.

Don't Eat Lunch Alone or at Your Desk

This is more than just a cliché. Use lunch and break time as an opportunity to build relationships and learn about what's "really" happening in and around the business. Many insights come from unplanned interactions and informal discussions.

Leverage Technology

Use collaboration platforms such as Slack and Teams Messaging as a way of increasing your informal interactions. By learning and using these available software tools efficiently, it can increase quick team interactions, replicating some of the benefits of being onsite together.

**Thriving in a Hybrid Team:
The Blueprint for Employees**

- Advocate by tracking progress toward your goals
- Seek support

- Build in-office relationships
- Focus on reestablishing effective relationships with your peers and cross-functional teams
- Segment your time
- Leverage technology to promote communication

Actions for Leaders

One of the toughest things to deal with as a leader in a hybrid environment is staying connected and communicating effectively with your team. If they are coming from a fully remote environment, they may feel comfortable and gotten in the habit of providing fewer updates, less information, and feeling a certain amount of autonomy in not seeing their manager daily.

Meet Weekly and Build Trust

Ask questions and encourage them to share their wins and frustrations. When we work with leaders, we encourage them to make sure they are taking time to include personal discussions and talk about life outside of work to help foster a good relationship built on trust. Once you have built that trust, so your employees feel supported by your management style, it becomes very important to call out their wins and provide good positive feedback. In the Gallup survey referenced at the beginning of this chapter, 80% of employees who said they received meaningful feedback in the past week were fully engaged – regardless of how many days they worked in the office.

Maximize In-Person Team Meetings

Have a clear agenda for the meeting and foster a good session. When in a hybrid environment, employees can often feel left out, not appreciated, or not recognized for their work. This could lead to them working scared and feeling insecure when they are not getting enough positive feedback from their manager. Another thing we encourage leaders to do when setting up an agenda is to prioritize the items from most important to least important. As the meeting leader, you are uniquely positioned to promote a positive meeting environment. Research has shown that the mood of the meeting leader is a good predictor of the eventual mood of the attendees. If possible, devote time at the beginning to focus on recognition, celebration, and appreciation – ideally, for the collective accomplishments of the team, but you can also target individual achievements.[3] Carve out time for every team member to speak, ideally early in the meeting to promote good discussion throughout. We also encouraged leaders at the start of each team meeting to have each member spend a few minutes highlighting what they are currently working on. When Ryan started doing this, Kendall loved this idea because it allowed her not only to remind Ryan of what she has been working on, but to communicate her projects to the other team members as well.

Prioritize Employee Appreciation

Show your gratitude to employees and make your appreciation genuine so it does not feel like you are "checking the boxes." Something simple and meaningful – such as a handwritten note or company swag such as company shirts or mugs – goes a long way to show appreciation. If you can, consider lunches on in-office days to create opportunities to connect. Use reunions and holiday parties to get the whole team back together at regular intervals.

Advocate for Your Employees

Companies tend to look at other companies in their market and follow their changes in the hybrid work environment. Many employees who have been hired in a hybrid or fully remote environment and have grown to love it could be working scared that one day those freedoms could disappear. It's important to know your team and know who might be most affected by a partial return-to-office policy, and to provide them with adequate support to make a transition. Be an advocate for your team. Take feedback and ask questions; how you can be better and what you can bring up to senior leadership that your team has concerns about. Just knowing you will do your best to advocate for your employees, whether it works or not, often goes a long way.

Establish Communication Norms

We encourage leaders to work with their team to come up with agreements on such practices as response times to emails and informal use of technology.[4] For example, how often should teams meet, what are the expectations of response time to emails, what are the expectations surrounding response time to informal messages such as Slack or Teams Messaging. Make sure that the team members have access and training regarding these technologies if necessary.

Establish Anchor Days

Depending on a department's needs, anchor days for hybrid workforces are only worthwhile if everyone from your team can be there. Therefore, when possible, attendance should be mandatory. For example, after Ryan met with Kendall and then with the team, Ryan decided that Tuesdays are anchor days where all team members will need to be in the office. The optimal number of days per week varies: a department whose work relies less on collaboration might find that one day per week is sufficient; other departments may need at least two or three days.[5]

Trust Your Team

After members of your team have established their ability to effectively work in a remote environment, don't micro-manage them. If you see they're "inactive" for a period on the messaging app, don't call them and ask why. With the transition from full-time in-office to hybrid, the 9-5 schedule doesn't necessarily exist. People work when it's convenient for them. Focus on deliverables, not the clock.

The most important function of a leader is to foster teamwork. This is of particular importance when working in a hybrid environment. Without real teamwork, a team can experience communication problems, backbiting, sabotage, job dissatisfaction, griping, low morale, and interpersonal conflicts.

Here are some additional ideas to help your hybrid team thrive:

- **Get out:** Hold retreats. Schedule an annual retreat for the whole team to build team spirit, talk about the team's vision and goals, renew commitment to the team, and get to know one another better.
- **Explore consensus:** Assess your decision-making style. How much or how often do you solicit your team members' ideas before arriving at important decisions? How unilateral are you? Find opportunities for using a consensus method – which usually results in better outcomes. Since moving to a hybrid model, changing his decision-making style has not been easy for Ryan.

At first, he went from being a control-oriented leader to a hands-off one. He thought that this was the way to build trust with his team. Like others, Ryan confused consensus decision-making with ineffective leadership. With time, Ryan found himself getting better at using a consensus decision-making approach. When there were important decisions to be made that affected the entire team, Ryan learned to hold team meetings on in-office days to discuss decisions and arrive at a consensus that makes sense for everyone. Over time, Ryan's team really began to appreciate their involvement in decision-making that affected their specific roles.

- **Encourage input:** Draw out quiet team members. As discussed in Chapter 3, leaders need to find ways to involve quiet team members in group discussions and decision-making and do so in a way that doesn't embarrass them. The use of open-ended questions (e.g., "How do you think the current anchor day is working out"), and reflective listening ("You feel that the deadlines that were imposed on the current project are too unrealistic?") often helps.

- **Value dissent:** Agree that it's OK to disagree. Managers are the most powerful motivators of healthy disagreement. They need to demonstrate that it is not only permissible, but valuable for team members to voice disagreement with them and with one another. Kendall realized that when Ryan conducted meetings during in-office days and allowed for disagreements, it made it easier for team members to also disagree with one another when they were working remotely, and they seemed to come to better decisions.

- **Celebrate wins:** Managers need to find ways to reward team accomplishments, celebrate the team, and share success with team members. Kendall and her peers appreciated that Ryan would always save what became known as "Ryan's celebrations" for in-office days. For example, when they completed a milestone for a particular project, he would congratulate everybody and have lunch brought in.

- **Encourage trust:** Managers must foster an environment of trust among their team members, as well as between themselves and their teams. This is especially true in a hybrid work environment that relies on both self-management and strong team collaboration. You can build trust in this environment by ensuring that all criticisms are constructive, and that everyone focuses on behaviors, not personalities. Managers need to make certain that they are honest with their people and are never found distorting the truth. It's better, in the long run, to say things that the team might not like hearing but need to hear.

- **Share credit:** When opportunities for external recognition occur, effective leaders don't hog the limelight – they spread it around among team members. This is of particular importance in a hybrid environment where employees have less visibility. Whether it's accepting an award from the local community, making a presentation to upper-level management, participating on highly visible committees in the organization, or getting named in the company newsletter, effective leaders make sure that everyone receives time in the limelight.

- **Clarify norms and expectations:** As mentioned earlier in this chapter, leaders should work collaboratively with their team members on clarifying the team's norms, so that everyone understands and agrees upon the standards of behavior. In this way, everyone understands what's expected of them.

Nobody should be working scared, worrying about whether other team members approve of what they are doing. Below are a few illustrations of norms:

- We attend all remote and in-office team meetings.
- We respond to emails within 24 hours and instant messaging within 2 hours.
- We leave video on during all remote meetings.
- We state our opinions even if they don't reflect the popular thing to say.

Ryan realized the importance of having team meetings occur on anchor days. He and the team agreed that team meetings should be mandatory even if someone cannot make it into the office on an anchor day. If, for whatever reason, a team member cannot come into the office, they should still be participating remotely. He realized that, at times, he was guilty of it himself and decided that he would always be in the office when it is an anchor day to set a positive role model.

- **Check in regularly:** Teams, like people, need to have periodic check-ups. Teams cannot afford to be complacent and just assume that everything is going great. Managers can help their teams by initiating a quarterly or semiannual self-examination where the team asks itself questions such as these:
  - What goals have we met?
  - Are we meeting our customers' needs?
  - What can we do to function better as a team?
  - How effective are our remote and in-office team meetings?
  - Is everyone on the team clear as to what's expected of them?

**Thriving in a Hybrid Environment:
The Blueprint for Leaders**

- Build trust through one-on-ones
- Maximize in-person meetings
- Provide support through change
- Clarify team norms
- Use anchor days to enhance collaboration
- Look for additional ways to enhance employee appreciation
- Trust your team
- Temperature check regularly

Chapter 5

Enduring a Restructuring/Downsizing

Ways to Keep Your Job and Your Peace of Mind

Restructuring, downsizing, layoffs, and reductions in force affect a staggering number of people. These business decisions cause employees in all types of jobs and industries to work scared.

Let's Look at Some Facts

- In March 2025, US employers reported approximately 1.6 million layoffs and discharges, representing a layoff rate of 1.0%.[1] The technology industry experienced more than 100,000 cuts in 2024.[2]
- An analysis revealed that women, who make up about 39% of the tech workforce, accounted for 48% of layoffs in this sector since September 2022.[3]
- Since 2023, the tech industry has eliminated over half a million jobs, reflecting significant workforce reductions across major companies.[4]
- It takes between 12 and 18 months for employee engagement levels to recover after layoffs, with longer recovery times observed for layoffs in 2023.[5]

- A study found that remote workers were 32% more likely than their in-office counterparts to feel anxious following layoff announcements.[6]

> **Chris Story**
>
> Chris is a 53-year-old research scientist employed by the government at a large biomedical research institution. His work involves conducting experiments, analyzing data, and developing new diagnostic and therapeutic methods. Chris and his fellow research scientists report to Debra, the Lab Manager. Chris has been with the government for 27 years. He joined the lab right out of graduate school and has steadily advanced within the institution. He finds his work both challenging and rewarding.
>
> One of the primary reasons Chris has stayed in his government role is job security. As he explains, "I could make more money in the private sector, but my wife and I decided that job security and, especially, health-care benefits were particularly important to us." Chris and his wife have an adult son with significant health issues. He adds, "In our case, our government insurance is the only coverage that will continue to insure our son beyond age 26. This security is very valuable to us."
>
> Although Chris's story may seem unique, it reflects many of the same concerns we hear from clients facing layoffs. They all want to take care of their families. And they share another common thread: they're all working scared. Leadership at the research institute believes staff cuts are necessary to control costs. As a result, many employees have been laid off in recent years. Just last year, 20 research scientists from Chris's lab were let go. Chris was close friends with several of them. Their departures left him feeling

> depressed and frustrated. These were talented scientists – why were they chosen? Why not others? Why not Chris?
>
> Debra has tried to reassure her team, telling them that their jobs are critical to the lab's success and are "about as secure as anyone can expect at this time." However, this has done little to ease Chris worries. He remains anxious, uncertain where he would go if he were to lose this job. Though he hates admitting it, he fears it's only a matter of time before he is let go. Chris is not alone in his anxiety. Debra has noticed a rise in workplace rumors that often become exaggerated and distorted. She has also observed a shift in team dynamics. Now, scientists are increasingly looking out for themselves, forming small cliques, and becoming less cooperative. This has led to more backbiting, less collaboration, and a noticeable decline in the lab's productivity, because time is wasted on gossip and speculation. The relationship among the research scientists is more like "sibling rivalry" than that of mentoring one another.

Actions for Employees

Like Chris, many of us may be afraid our job will be eliminated. Working successfully in a climate of fear presents both emotional and practical issues. In this chapter we'll look at strategies to help deal with the fear and potentially save your job.

Upskill and Reskill

One way of guarding against being the next person to be laid off is to build your skills. This is no time to freeze up. Instead:

- Focus your efforts on upskilling and reskilling. Upskilling involves improving your skill set in your current job while reskilling involves developing new cross-functional skills. Through reskilling, you will become more capable of moving into a new role if your current position is eliminated.

- Identify where you can develop additional skills to better position yourself to be more valuable to your company. This can range from formal classroom training and executive coaching to online self-study.
- Stay informed and proactive regarding new developments in your field, news in your industry, and upcoming events in your professional associations.
- Think back to the last performance review meeting that you had with your manager. Remember what you were told about your strengths and weaknesses. Develop a plan for mitigating your weaknesses.

Tap Your Network

Another way of making sure you keep your job is to reach out for help. Here are some tips:

- Go through *all* your contacts: coworkers (present and past), friends, family. Identify the people who could be helpful.
- Contact (and, if necessary, reintroduce yourself) to them and share your current situation.
- Ask each of them for *at least* one additional name. In this way, you are systematically expanding your network based on trusted relationships.
- Reach out to these new contacts and don't be shy about asking for help. Keep in mind that people may be resistant if you ask them for a job, but they will be open if you ask them for advice.

Chris initially focused on his closest work colleagues and a former mentor. Only when he mentioned it to a neighbor did he realize the importance of a broader network. That neighbor suggested two people in Chris's field who were looking to expand their teams.

Be Aware of Rumors, But Don't Believe Everything You Hear

Rumors occur simply because we're human and we need to do something, anything, to relieve our fears. You can expect to hear rumors anywhere – in online chats or at the office in the hallway, restroom, cafeteria, or parking lot. The rumors themselves hardly ever involve employees' names. Instead, rumors are about functional areas – "I heard that customer service is going to get trimmed, but sales and engineering are going to be saved." Don't ignore rumors; they are an important source of information. They will help you stay informed. No matter how bizarre or painful, rumors will help you to better gauge your company's cultural temperature. But don't get obsessed by them. Listen to everything, but don't believe everything you hear. Always consider the source. We often tell our clients that when you hear a rumor from someone, stop and ask yourself:

- Does this person have access to credible information?
- Can I trust this person to tell me the truth?
- Does this individual have anything to gain from telling me this?

If the answers make you uneasy, then you need to verify the information with trustworthy sources such as co-workers who are your friends. We've often been asked by our clients, *"Does it make sense to check rumors with my manager?"* Although the answer depends somewhat on your personal relationship with your manager, you should know that this is usually a tricky area. If your manager is involved in making difficult downsizing decisions, they can't say anything to you. From a legal standpoint, managers have to be careful about what they say, especially when terminations are involved. But that doesn't mean you have to keep totally silent. You can certainly discuss the rumor with family and friends – and you should. If downsizing eventually affects you, and you haven't at least prepared family and friends for the possibility, they can be devastated. Besides, they are your best source of support. Discussing rumors and fears with those we're closest to is an excellent way of reducing fear.

Chris continues to listen to the rumors, but he also takes into consideration their source before taking them seriously. He realizes that his primary concern must always be his level of job performance, and he cannot let "doing rumors" interfere with doing his work.

Generate Your Unique Value Proposition (UVP) to Articulate Your Value

Another way to be proactive is to develop what is called a Unique Value Proposition (UVP). A UVP is typically used by a business as a concise statement that explains why a customer should choose a specific product or service over its competitors. It articulates the unique benefits, solutions, and value that a company or offering provides, emphasizing what makes it stand out in the market. We adapted this marketing technique to help our clients stand out in their workplace. In such cases, your UVP explains how you provide distinct value to your organization. It describes the benefits your organization derives from having you as an employee, and how you differ from other employees. The version we use with clients is shown in Figure 5.1. Try creating your own UVP by answering the following three questions:

(1) **Who** depends on me most, and what do they need from me? (e.g., key internal and external customers, my manager, my peers)

(2) **What** skills, knowledge, and wisdom help me meet those needs? (e.g., expertise, training, track record)

(3) **How** do I deliver value that makes a real difference? (innovative thinking, temperament, professional network, personal values)

Once you have developed your UVP, share it with your network. This becomes your brand; embody your UVP. Soon, your UVP will

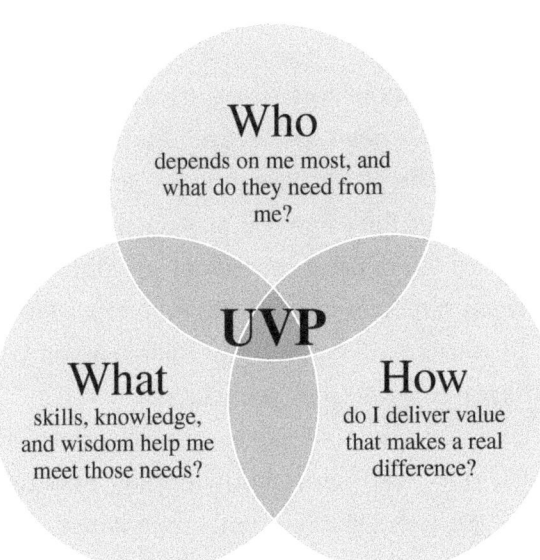

Figure 5.1 Components of a Unique Value Proposition

explain clearly to your manager, and to other key stakeholders in your company, why you are valuable to your organization and, hopefully, why they cannot afford to lose you.

We worked with Chris over several sessions as he worked to keep his job. He developed a UVP he was proud to share. Once he had his UVP, Chris did a few things with the intention of staying within the research institution. First, he updated his resume by incorporating his UVP. He highlighted specific benefits of his recent research projects for which he received special recognition from his Section Chief. Second, he described how his 27 years of service combined with his innovative thinking helped him to prioritize, work across departments, and think strategically. Third, Chris spoke with Debra about his UVP to stay visible. You can find Chris's UVP in the Appendix at the end of this chapter.

Acknowledge the Full Range of Emotions You Experience

Whenever any organization downsizes, it violates two fundamental motivating precepts: the need for security and the desire for justice. Downsizing poses a threat to the survivors' sense of security since now they're afraid that they may be among the next to go. It also violates their desire for fairness; survivors usually identify with the laid off employees rather than with the company. Moreover, survivors find it difficult to understand how their company could be so callous and disloyal to those they let go.

It's important that you, as a survivor, not ignore or deny your natural feelings: only through acknowledging and understanding them can you hope to reestablish your own sense of security and fairness. Take advantage of the support of others such as co-workers, friends, family, and managers. At the same time, learn to recognize the array of thoughts and feelings brought on by downsizing, and give yourself time to process them. These feelings may include:

- **Sadness.** It's depressing to see your friends and co-workers being asked to leave the company.
- **Distrust.** You now wonder whether your organization or management can be trusted to keep their word.
- **Fear.** You become afraid of making mistakes and taking risks.
- **Anger.** You feel angry that your employer has made these decisions, and especially when it impacts you and your co-workers.
- **Nervousness.** You become preoccupied with the fear that you might be the next to go, which is unsettling and distracting.
- **Guilt.** You feel guilty that you kept your job while your co-workers have lost theirs.
- **Confusion.** You experience a type of confusion known as "role ambiguity." You're unsure about your new responsibilities, and what management now expects of you.
- **Relief.** You feel thankful and relieved that you still are employed.
- **Anticipation.** You feel that things have settled down for the moment, but you anticipate and worry about more layoffs coming.

You may be experiencing some or all these feelings. Our clients often share that they experience a roller coaster of emotions. They may start to feel at peace only later to feel anxious or sad. That is normal. What's important is that you treat your emotions as useful information and find ways to manage them constructively. That is what we will cover next.

Plan for the Worst, But Hope for Something Better

We have many clients who live in fear that they'll be laid off. Chris told us that "I wake up each day, scared to go to work, because I'll find out that I'm going to be out of a job." We helped Chris and others cope with the fears they are experiencing by using what we call the "worst-case scenario." We asked Chris to consider what is the worst possible thing that could happen to him if he were laid off. Chris answered that he was scared that he'd never find another job that's as good as the one he has. We then said to Chris, "Let's imagine, for a moment, that this really happened to you. What would you do?" Chris thought for a while and started to realize that he has a few close friends who are employed and could put him in touch with contacts they have at their companies. Lastly, we asked Chris, "What's the probability that this worst-case scenario could actually happen to you?" Chris thought for a while and then said, "it's not as likely as I thought," and obviously started feeling better.

If you can anticipate and manage the worst-case scenario, you're on the road to coping with your fears and your stress successfully. Remember this – considering the worst-case scenario will put things in perspective for you.

Navigating a Restructuring/Downsizing: The Blueprint for Employees

- Upskill and reskill
- Tap your network for people who can be helpful
- Be aware of the grapevine
- Generate your Unique Value Proposition (UVP)
- Acknowledge the feelings
- Consider worst-case scenarios

Actions for Leaders

People who survive a downsizing are in a very difficult position and are undoubtedly working scared. They usually have more work to do, and they are expected to do it in an atmosphere of fear and distrust. Is it any wonder their productivity slips? No one should be expected to cope with this situation without help from their manager. It is the manager's job to help employees deal with the negative emotions and to find new commitment and motivation for doing quality work. Now, let's discuss some of the things leaders can do before, during, and after a layoff has taken place.

Use Your Employee's UVP to Advocate

Encourage your employees to generate their Unique Value Proposition. Work with them to refine it based on your observations. Then, use their UVP as a topic in your discussions with your own leadership, emphasizing the unique contribution your team members make to the organization. One of the most important things that you can do as a leader is to stand up for your employees during a restructuring or downsizing.

Meanwhile, create visibility for your team members. Give them opportunities to shine such as making presentations to upper-level management. During times of downsizing, this is a critical moment to make sure your team is seen. Finally, it's extremely important to let your employees know what you are doing on their behalf.

Chris's leader demonstrated deep commitment to protecting her team. Debra decided to delay her retirement with the explicit intention of supporting her team through the uncertain period. In addition, she leveraged her political skills, meeting with officials and regulators to promote the work on her team and its impact on the research institution. Through her clear messaging and persistence, she was able to get commitments to prolonged funding. Chris told us that "It's not a permanent solution, but it increased our confidence in Debra and brought some relief to the fears we had."

Provide As Much Information As Possible

At this critical time, leaders need to be perceived as the calm at the center of the storm. More than anything else, this means communicating as much information as possible to your employees. First, you must confidently explain to employees what has happened, why it's happened, and why the organization is on the right track. Employees are more willing to accept immediate injustices if they can see how their organization's actions will contribute to long-term benefits for themselves and others.

Second, you must find ways of heading off rumors. Employees will talk about what they believe to be is going on in the organization. If they're not given real information, then they'll simply create and pass on rumors. Debra installed a "rumor board" outside her office. If Chris hears a rumor, he can write it up and post it on the rumor board. Within 24 hours, Debra posts the real facts pertaining to the issue next to the rumor. Rumors spread quickly. Therefore, it's important that employees be told the truth, even if the truth is that studies are being conducted and no final decisions have been made yet.

Third, you must clarify what you expect from each employee from now on. The survivors are worried about their increased workloads and unfamiliar job responsibilities. Debra met individually and privately with all the research scientists to explain exactly what each of them will be expected to do, how they will do it, and with whom they'll interact. You must also keep in mind that the survivors are largely entering what is essentially a new organization. Simply informing them of their new responsibilities is not enough. You need to explain, in detail, how they will be helped to adapt to their new tasks and responsibilities through coaching, training, and mentoring.

Provide Compassionate Support

Following a downsizing, those employees who survive need extra support. Fortunately, there are several things you can do, as a leader, during this stressful period to provide compassion. For one thing, let your employees know that you realize the hardships imposed on them by the downsizing. It also helps to meet with employees in small groups and individually to give them an opportunity to vent their feelings of frustration, shock, sorrow, guilt, and/or anger. Many employees need time and help to work through their negative feelings before they will be ready to move forward constructively. Emphasize how their expertise will contribute to future departmental and company goals.

Compassion for those employees who have to leave is critical, too. How they are treated will have a lasting effect on those who stay. It's the first and probably most important impression of the downsizing for the employees who stay. As a leader, do everything in your power to see that the layoffs are handled professionally and compassionately.

Restore Smart Risk-Taking with a Reassuring Message

During layoffs, be prepared for your employees to become risk averse. They are scared to make a mistake that could end up causing them to lose their jobs. Their reduction in risk-taking will reduce job performance. We often remind our clients that it is essential to tackle this proactively. You need to reassure your team members that smart risk-taking is necessary to drive performance and that you, as their leader, will have their backs.

> **Navigating a Restructuring/Downsizing:
> The Blueprint for Leaders**
>
> - Use your employee's UVP to advocate
> - Communicate clearly and often
> - Provide compassionate support
> - Restore smart risk-taking

Appendix: Chris's Unique Value Proposition (UVP) as an Example in Action

We worked with Chris to follow the process outlined in Figure 5.2.

In **Step 1**, Chris answered the three core questions of the UVP. He generated the following responses:

> **(1) Who** depends on me most, and what do they need from me? (e.g., key internal and external customers, my manager, my peers)
> - Section Chief
> - Manager, Debra

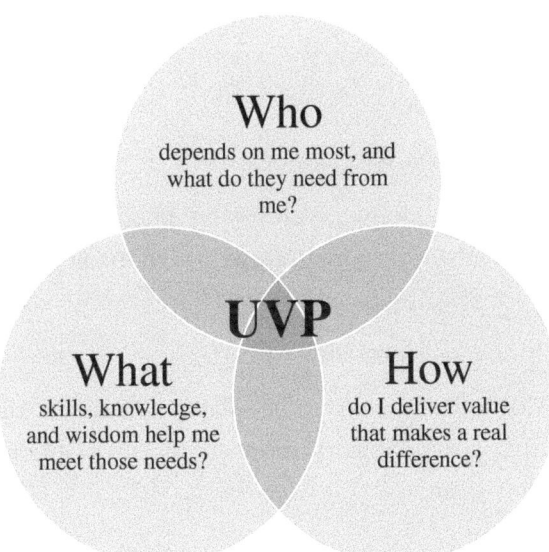

Figure 5.2 The Three-Step Process for Creating Your UVP

Enduring a Restructuring/Downsizing

- Review Committee that evaluates scientific productivity and allocates funding
- Policymakers and government officials
- Partner research institutes (universities, hospitals, etc. with whom we coordinate research)

(2) What skills, knowledge, and wisdom help me meet those needs? (e.g., expertise, training, track record)

- Research expertise in infectious diseases and advanced therapeutics method
- 27 years of institutional knowledge
- Prioritization skills/smart risk-taking/knowing which projects to tackle
- Project management/experimental process
- Data analytics
- Broad professional network

(3) How do I deliver value that makes a real difference? (innovative thinking, temperament, professional network, personal values)

- Innovative problem-solver
- Continuous learner (follows trends in the industry, and spots opportunities that are occurring in other industries)
- Visionary thinking
- Resilient and adaptive to change
- Commitment to the mission of the organization

In **Step 2**, we focused on all the answers Chris generated and prioritized the most important elements to each question. He provided the following input:

- Who: Section Chief + Manager
- What: Prioritization skills + Institutional knowledge
- How: Innovative problem-solver + Continuous learner

Finally, we spent time on **Step 3** to combine the answers into a single sentence. This was an iterative process. Over time, he drafted the following sentence and felt it captured his UVP:

> *"My value to this organization is that I am uniquely able to spot innovative solutions and to focus on the most impactful research to advance the mission of our institution."*

Chapter 6

Prevailing Through Mergers and Acquisitions

Techniques to Face the Unknown and Find Your Place Again

Imagine this scenario. You heard the rumors for the first time about three months ago, but you didn't really think it would happen. Last Friday it was announced – a large corporation has acquired your employer, a company that has been such an important part of your life for the past nine years. You have so many questions and so few answers.

- Will I be able to keep my job?
- Will the organization's expectations of me change?
- Will I be transferred to another location?
- Will I be demoted?
- Will I lose my accumulated benefits?
- Who will I be reporting to in the new organization?
- How will decisions get made?
- Will that job assignment or promotion I was promised be honored?
- Will my pay be affected?
- How will redundancies in staff positions be handled?

If you were in this situation, how would you feel? If you *are* in this kind of situation, *how do you feel?* Working scared? If it's any comfort, you are not alone.

Let's Look at Some Facts

McKinsey reports for all of 2024, the global value of deals over $25 million rose 12% to $3.4 trillion, from $3.1 trillion a year before. The number of companies changing hands increased 8% (to 7,784, from 7,206 in 2023). Average global deal value rose 4% (to $443 million from $424 million in 2023) as macroeconomic conditions improved and as dealmakers – toughened by repeated rounds of volatility – grew more inured to geopolitical tensions and political transitions.[1]

Companies use M&As as a strategy to achieve organizational growth, access new markets, gain efficiencies, and stay competitive. Many companies merge or acquire simply to survive.

A word about terminology: throughout the chapter we will be using the terms M&A, merger, and acquisition interchangeably. There is a tendency for the smaller company to view the transaction as a merger, whereas the larger organization typically views the same deal as an acquisition. Our emphasis in this chapter will be on the company that has been acquired by a larger organization. Nevertheless, from an employee perspective the issues are similar. No matter which side of the fence they are on, employees are working scared.

> **Adam's Story**
> Adam has been working for a manufacturer of consumer products for the past nine years. Adam had always loved working for the company because of their interest in developing employees. It was

a profitable company where the employees liked to describe the company as "world class." Many of the 12,000 employees worked in facilities that could best be described as "pastoral settings located in the middle of the woods," and this seemed to fit the culture of the organization. Then came the announcement: they were being acquired by a much larger organization – an aggressive competitor, no less.

When Adam looks back on it now, he can identify five stages that the M&A process went through.[2]

Stage 1: The Official News Drops. "Everyone knew where they were when they heard about the merger for the first time. Some employees were in their cars, and they heard it on the radio, others were in meetings. I was in my office. I remember looking around, feeling like all the blood had just drained from my face. 'Shock' and 'disbelief' are the words that come to mind. I started to think about how much larger the organization was that we were merging with. I knew that many of the things about my organization's culture that meant so much to me were going to change. I was scared!"

Stage 2: Preoccupation. "All of us were obsessed with the merger. It was all we could think about; it was all we would talk about. It certainly did not help our productivity. I remember staring at my computer looking at all the reports I put together for management and project reports and thinking that all my past work could now be meaningless. Tension and chaos were in the air as we waited for the conquerors to arrive."

Stage 3: The Culture Clash. "They arrived. Some key new organizational members were added to the organizational chart.

(continued)

> *(continued)*
>
> 'Arrogance' was the word that comes to mind. They were going to show us how to really run a company. There were big differences between the way the two companies did business, and it became quite clear that they wanted their way to become our way."
>
> **Stage 4: Let the Purging Begin.** "We were told that as a result of the merger, there would be a reduction in force of around 20%. They kept stressing that 80% of us would not be affected, but of course, 100% of us were worried. Some of our best talent left the company on their own, and others seemed to be let go for reasons we never really understood."
>
> **Stage 5: Merging and Emerging.** "We realized that we were survivors, and it was time to get away from the we-versus-they, the attack-and-defend, and the win-versus-lose mentality if the merger was going to be successful. I also remember reading about M&As and realizing, according to many experts, that 'people problems' had a greater influence on the long-term success of mergers and acquisitions than financial problems. I was determined not to be one of the people problems."

Actions for Employees

How can you be successful through a merger and acquisition and keep from working scared? Here are some actions you can take.

Expect Change in Culture, Role, and Co-Workers

If you thought there were a lot of changes going on before the merger took place, just wait – you haven't seen anything yet. There will be changes in the organizational culture, your job, and your co-workers. Change can no longer be thought of as a short-term reaction to a crisis or new competition, but rather a fact of today's organizational life. For additional information about the changing workplace see Chapter 1. Let's talk about four types of changes.

1. **Changes in Organizational Culture.** There are going to be different priorities within the new organization. What was important in the past may not be as important now. There may be a new emphasis on customer service or quality. Values and traditions will probably change. For example, employees often complain that after a merger there was an overemphasis on profits at the expense of people. It should not be surprising, considering that top management is trying to prove they were right to suggest the merger to begin with. You will also see changes in the way decisions are made. Expect mixed messages regarding how much you will be involved in decision-making. On the one hand, there may be a lot of listening and shared decision-making. On the other, there could be very autocratic decisions handed down by top management in response to the pressures of profitability.

2. **Changes in Your Role.** Your job title may not change, but your responsibilities and actual job duties probably will. Be prepared to have changes move in one of two directions. The first is that you will have less responsibility. Instead of supervising the work, you are now the one doing the work. It may be frustrating to realize that you have just taken what seems to be a step backward. Some employees report that they feel they are doing the jobs of people who were two levels below them in the old company. But a step backward in your job responsibilities may in fact be a step forward regarding job security or additional opportunities in a much larger post-merger company. On the other

hand, you could have more responsibility. The new organization is running leaner than before. This is a real opportunity to show your talent to the new organization. Get your new role clarified, find out what is expected of you, and exceed their expectations. The reality may be that your opportunities are much greater after the acquisition than they were before.

3. **Changes in Your Co-Workers.** Friends and colleagues you enjoyed working with on a day-to-day basis may have been transferred or left the company. Get to know your new colleagues, share your job histories, and look for things that you have in common. If you have a new manager from the other company, try to clarify as best as you can what is expected of you. Use your new manager to help provide your education about the other company. Ask questions. Learn the rules related to customers and other departments.

4. **Change in Who You Report To.** Three months ago, Tom came over from the other company to manage the group that Adam was part of for six years. Adam's previous boss for the entire six years took early retirement.

At first Adam was apprehensive, but now he thinks having a new boss is one of the better things that has happened to him since the merger. Why? Because Tom has answers. He has given Adam a tremendous education in the history and culture of the other company that he never would have been able to get in such a short time otherwise. Because Adam was genuinely interested and willing to ask the right questions, he was able to function more successfully in the new organization.

So, what's your bottom line? Expect change, be flexible, and adapt. Organizational decision-makers should see you as one who adapts well to change no matter where it occurs. Adjusting to change is critical to your success. Being inflexible, assuming there is no better way of doing things than the way they have been done in the past, is a sure way of failing. To really succeed in the new company, you need to do more than accommodate change. You should be seen as a change agent. Employees who respond to change by saying, "Things are going fine. If it ain't broke, don't fix it," are going to be stuck. To move ahead, you should be saying, "If it ain't broke let's break it and make it better."

Learn How to Reduce Stress

Change causes stress. Seeing your company swallowed up by another is stressful, indeed, and can affect you in many ways. M&As create eight specific sources of stress:

1. **Role overload.** You are told, as discussed earlier, the organization must run "lean and mean" because of the merger. You understand how that may help the short-term bottom line for the organization, but it is creating high levels of stress. You feel that you are assigned more work than you can possibly handle.

2. **Role ambiguity.** In the past, you were clear on what the organization expected of you. Because of all the changes going on in the organization, you no longer have a clear idea of what is expected of you.

3. **Role conflict.** You are used to doing your job in a certain way and have been quite productive in the past. Now, however, employees in the company that acquired yours are acting like the "conquering heroes." They are telling you how to do things in a manner that you believe may not work well in your organization.

4. **Fear of job loss.** You realize it is quite common for merged and acquired companies to downsize. You have survived so far, but you are worried that you could be next.

5. **Politics and power struggles.** Everybody seems to be jockeying for position. Projects that were moving along now seem to have lost their funding. Politics rather than job performance seems to be the daily concern of co-workers, and it becomes very difficult to get your job done. Time and effort seem to be continually wasted on corporate politics.

6. **Infrequent feedback.** Amid all the turmoil, you are really putting in the effort and trying to do a good job. But you are given very little feedback about your job performance, resulting in greater stress.

7. **Autocratic leadership.** You seem to be left out of the decision-making loop on many issues that you were always part of in the past. The right words have always been there from the acquiring company, but the actions do not follow. You may be part of the "new family," but you are being treated like a stranger. It seems that the leaders demand miracles but do not provide the necessary support.

8. **Career uncertainty.** You no longer feel that the career opportunities that once existed are still realistic. There seem to be fewer opportunities for career growth than ever before. Exacerbating the eight stressors described above is the general organizational climate of ambiguity and uncertainty that takes over. This climate and the resulting information vacuum exist for several reasons:

   - Top management feels a need to be discreet in case the merger is not finalized.

   - Management does not have a clear sense of direction.

- Management itself lacks information about the impact of the merger.
- Everyone, including leadership, is suffering from fear of the unknown.

Stress and uncertainty are facts of organizational life during M&As. So, what can you do? Learn how to manage what cannot be avoided. Here are some specific things you can do to manage the stress.

Learn simple meditation. Herbert Benson of Harvard Medical School demystified the concept of meditation in his technique, The Relaxation Response.[3] Adam has really been stressed out since his company was acquired. After learning the Benson technique, he decided to try it. Here is his routine:

- Adam finds a quiet room and sits in a comfortable position.
- He closes his eyes and takes a "what happens, happens" attitude.
- He begins to deeply relax all muscles. He does this by tensing and then relaxing each muscle group, starting with his fists, progressing up his arms to his head, and down his torso to his feet. He tries to keep his muscles completely relaxed.
- He breathes through his nose, concentrating on his breathing. Then he says the word "one" silently to himself, on every out-breath. (It could be any word or phrase; it's simply a device to keep his mind from wandering.)
- When distracting thoughts come into his mind, he simply allows them to "pass through" while he concentrates on repeating the word "one."
- Adam does not worry about how deeply he is relaxed while meditating. He knows that he cannot force the relaxing effects of meditation. He takes what he can get.

Adam has found that he feels a sense of calm and relaxation after meditating. It only takes about 10 minutes, but it seems to give him some control over his reaction to the various stressors he has been encountering at work.

Several studies have found that people who meditate recover from stress more rapidly than nonmeditators.

Strive for balance. Adam's initial reaction to the M&A was to eat, think, breathe, and talk work. He thought the best thing he could do was to put off vacations and social events and instead throw himself into work. He was wrong. That only made the stress worse.

Don't put your life on hold. Take planned vacations, go-to special events that you look forward to, and exercise regularly. If you don't already have an exercise program, start one. In addition to the health and fitness benefits, physical exercise reduces stress.

Change your thinking. One of the most powerful methods of dealing with stress is analyzing and changing the way you think. The way you think about stress can make stress worse. We often make several mental errors that contribute to our stress level during M&As that include:

- **Selective perception.** Once the M&A takes place, it is easy for you to assume that the organization is now a terrible place to work. You then start looking for all the reasons why it is a terrible place and ignore all evidence to the contrary.

- **Overgeneralizing.** "Since our company was acquired, I no longer have any supervisory responsibilities. Therefore, I must have been worthless as a supervisor." This is an overgeneralization based on only one situation. The decision to take away supervisory responsibilities may have nothing to do with your abilities as a supervisor but was simply companywide policy.

- **Catastrophizing.** You may tend to blow the significance of negative events way out of proportion. "The way our company was before we were acquired was the best company I will ever work for. My job was the greatest job I will ever have. I'll never have another job that good. I'll never be as happy at work again."

How you *think* will determine how you behave. Here are some ways of changing the way you think:

- **Changing your self-talk.** Examine carefully what you say inside your head. Notice those times when you are catastrophizing and blowing things out of proportion. How can you shift this? Here are a few examples of positive self-talk.
    - "I have had difficult situations at work before, and I have always done a good job of handling them. I know I can handle this one."
    - "I'm going to concentrate on making the best out of the situation. I won't waste time worrying about things I have no control over."
    - "It seems bad now, but this could end up being the best thing that ever happened to me with regard to work. There may be new opportunities. Let's wait and see what happens."
- **Consider worst case.** Ask yourself, what is the worst possible thing that could happen to me? Are you going to die because your company was acquired by another? No. Are you going to lose your health? No. Are you going to go to jail? No. Are you going to lose your job? Maybe. Now you have hit on the worst possible outcome. If you can accept this worst-case scenario, you are on the road to dealing with the situation successfully.

You can now put things in perspective. You may even be saying to yourself that you were thinking about looking for another job anyway, and in the past whenever you changed jobs it was always a step up. You have now created a much healthier scenario.

- **Visualize your actions.** Imagining yourself in a stressful situation and rehearsing how you are going to handle it. It involves practicing an upcoming stressful event in your head. Here again, the premise of the technique is that your attitudes and thoughts are going to affect your behaviors. The more positive and successful your thoughts are, the more effective the actual behaviors. Suppose you must make a presentation to the acquiring company's top management team. It could have a tremendous impact on your career. Try to visualize the event in detail, starting with what the room is like and what you're wearing. Run through the entire situation in your mind. Picture yourself being asked difficult questions and handling them successfully. Repeat this mental rehearsal several times until you begin to feel more comfortable with the upcoming presentation.

- **Become part of the solution, not the problem.** No matter how large or small it is, the company you work for often becomes an important part of your personal identity. When that company is acquired by another larger organization, it loses its original identity, and you therefore may feel part of your identity has been lost too. The five stages of grief developed by psychiatrist Elisabeth Kübler-Ross are also applicable in this case:

    - **Denial:** When Adam first heard the rumor that the merger was about to take place, he refused to believe it. He continued to deny that the merger was happening. Somehow, he believed his company would thwart off the merger.

Even after the merger took place, he convinced himself that his company would be allowed to remain independent.

- **Anger:** Then his reaction turned to anger. His energy now focused on the "evil empire" that was in the process of taking them over. How dare they destroy his world like that!

- **Bargaining:** Adam decided he must try to do something about it. He and some of his colleagues met with several key players from the other company. Their goal was to bargain with them to leave their part of the organization alone.

- **Depression:** Adam began to realize that all the bargaining in the world was not going to persuade the other organization to leave them alone; they wanted complete integration. Adam and his co-workers were depressed. The old company was really gone, and they were going to miss it. They also realized that many others felt the same way, and they decided it was okay to mourn their loss. They decided to throw a rest-in-peace party. Everyone got T-shirts printed with "RIP" and the old company logo. They told stories, reminisced, laughed, and cried. When the party was over, most felt they had said goodbye to the old company.

- **Acceptance:** It was time to face reality. Adam began having a more positive attitude toward the other company. He became part of the solution, rather than part of the problem, by looking for ways the companies could more effectively integrate his department.

- **Set goals.** You may not know exactly how the merger will affect you, but now is the time to keep yourself motivated by setting goals for the near future. It could be helpful for you to use the AIME Model for Change to guide your efforts, which was described in Chapter 1. Using this framework can help you to take steady, intentional steps so that change feels less overwhelming. Here are a few points to keep in mind when setting goals:

- **Be specific.** Adam knew that if he was going to keep himself motivated, he couldn't just decide he was going to "do his best." He set very specific key job goals and gave each one a deadline. He kept these goals in a file that he could easily and regularly access.

- **Stretch yourself.** Adam made sure his goals were reasonably difficult to achieve – difficult but not impossible. He knew that, in this fashion, he would not only be more productive but also get a sense of accomplishment from achieving his goals.

- **Measure your results.** If the goal-setting process was going to keep Adam motivated, he knew he had to make sure his goals were measurable. Adam set his goals based on what he wanted to accomplish over the next three to six months. Then he set short-term weekly goals so he could measure how he was doing along the way.

- **Be a positive force.** Throw your energies into being positive rather than focusing on what is upsetting and frustrating. Don't continually look for what is wrong, but search for the positive. Often, employees report that M&A changes are more positive than they originally anticipated.

- **Stick it out or move on.** At what point do you decide it is not worth it, that it's time to put your resume together? Immediately after an M&A, there are typically going to be short-term setbacks, but they should not be the basis for deciding to quit. The larger concern ought to be what you think is going to happen one to two years down the road. Short-term problems may be corrected, and your career could be back on track. It is important to understand that impulsive career moves made from panic or other emotions are often poor moves. You do not want to make career decisions out of panic. As we have seen, during the initial phases of an M&A, you may find yourself angry and depressed. Now is not the time to make long-term career decisions. Impulsive decisions often lead to poor consequences. Take the long view: What is best for you over the next couple of years?

On the other hand, you may feel that the changes are unacceptable, and you cannot be a positive force in helping the merger along. It may be time to move on.

But you want to ask yourself if the new job will enhance at least one of the five following characteristics:

1. More responsibility
2. Substantially higher pay
3. More interesting daily activities
4. Less stress and anxiety
5. More psychologically rewarding

The bottom line is, don't psychologically remove yourself from your present position or announce your plans to leave until you have something else lined up. Make sure your productivity remains high. Even if you have already decided to find another job, you are going to need references from your current employer.

- **Get on their wavelength** Let's face it, whether you like it or not, the merger is a fact. To be successful, you should start learning as much as you can about the other side. Adam decided to stay with the organization and has made a concerted effort to get to know the organization that acquired his company. The first thing he did was change his attitude. Before the acquisition,

Adam had always looked down on the other company; after all, they were a competitor. Now, however, he realized it was time to start looking for the positive in both the other company and its people. For the first time he realized they were all on the same team. Next, Adam started a crash course on learning as much about the other company as he could. He obtained past annual reports, company brochures, and newsletters. He even went to the human resource department and asked for employee on-boarding materials. He started talking to employees from the other company. He asked questions to learn as much as he could about the other company's history and its culture. Finally, Adam volunteered to serve on merger transition and integration teams. As one vice president who has been through nine acquisitions put it, "Those individuals who achieve success during M&As seem to be able to go with the flow." Adam realized that by being flexible and showing an eagerness to learn about the other side, he not only increased his chances for success but was also turning the merger process into a genuine growth experience for himself. It also allowed him to get to know the other side and allowed the other side to get to know him.

Prevailing Through Mergers and Acquisitions: The Blueprint for Employees

- Adapt to change
- Reduce stress
- Become part of the solution
- Stick it out or move on
- Get on their wavelength

Actions for Leaders

Leaders on both sides of the merger will find these strategies helpful during the difficult transition period:

Overcommunicate

Make a conscious decision to communicate more than you think is necessary. Don't exceed the available facts, but make sure you communicate continually, with timely and comprehensive information. Keep in mind that you will likely have to repeat the same important message multiple times for people to digest the content. The more informed employees are, the more favorable their attitudes toward the merger will be. Sharing the "why" behind the deal and giving clear purpose-driven communication will help accelerate trust and reduce attrition on the part of employees during the M&A.[4]

Soon after the merger was announced, Adam found that different leaders worked through the process in very different ways. Tom seemed to do an outstanding job of communicating with his work group. In group meetings, one-on-one, and in writing, he let them know what was happening. He gave them frequent updates, and he was always honest about organizational changes. In short, Tom was able to counter any unfounded rumors by sharing information freely.

Become a Role Model

Publicize anything the two firms do together to showcase how they are working in tandem during the merger. In this way, you become a spokesperson for the merger and a role model for a positive attitude. Share everything you know about the acquiring firm's goals, values, and philosophies. Become a teacher in the characteristics of the acquiring firm and actively manage the employee experience. When employees are actively engaged in the journey, they can become powerful advocates of the M&A.[5]

Remember, as a leader, you have the greatest impact on what employees will think of the merger and how they will act. Your goal should be to help them let go of the past by getting them enthusiastic about the future.

Exhibit Leadership

Don't start playing it too safe. Remain a steadfast leader and a decision-maker. Structure your employees' work and tell them what is expected of them. Make sure you let them know where they stand and reward them for taking the initiative and not just playing it safe.

Make sure that the strategic preparation for the merger goes beyond the financial and business aspects of the transaction and focuses on the human implications as well. Remember, it is most often the "people problems" that cause M&As to fail.

Involve the Employees in the Change

The more you can get your employees involved in the changes, the more accepting they will be. Involve your employees on integration teams. If your department is merging with a similar department in the other organization, ask employees to help. Allow them to share with you their ideas about the most effective ways of merging the two departments. Allow departmental employees to meet and put together what they consider to be their greatest strengths that will contribute to the success of the new department.

Become their coach

Give employees a chance to air their fears. Help provide support by making a conscious effort to be as visible as possible and answering all questions as soon as you can. Serve as a counselor and good listener to show you value their opinions and ideas. Let the employees know that you realize that fear and anxiety are often an unfortunate byproduct of M&As. Wherever these feelings come from, let your employees know that you are willing to listen and discuss them.

Treat the ones who leave with dignity and those who stay with respect

How you treat the leavers will affect the stayers. It significantly colors their overall impression of the M&A. In addition, employees who stay often feel guilty about being "survivors." Make sure that you acknowledge the experience that the stayers bring to the firm. Let them know that you respect and appreciate their years of service and that their experience and expertise will help make the new company more successful.

Don't act like a conquering hero

If you are a leader from the acquiring firm, you must be very careful about the impression you make with employees from the other company. Adam told us "some of the managers from the other company acted like they were the conquering heroes. They were going to show us how naive we were about the way we did our jobs. There was only one right way, and it was their way. We were constantly told how flexible we needed to be, but they were totally inflexible." Remember, acting like a conquering hero will have a negative effect on how you communicate, how you lead, and ultimately, how successful you are at managing during the M&A.

Adam felt Tom did an outstanding job in this area. He reported, "Tom calmed many people down. He gave talks to several work groups in our facility, and we began to realize that the people from the other firm were not bad people. We began to realize that we were all in this thing together."

> **Prevailing Through Mergers and Acquisitions: The Blueprint for Leaders**
>
> - Prioritize communication
> - Model positive leadership
> - Involve employees
> - Be available
> - Offer dignity and respect
> - Show empathy

Chapter 7

Building a Sense of Security Amidst Economic Turmoil

What to Do to Stay Grounded, Prepared, and Productive

Economic fluctuations, policy changes, industry shifts, and market volatility can leave employees feeling anxious, demoralized, and uncertain in their roles. Even for the best performers who feel their job is safe, the fear of what might happen can erode focus and motivation. This nagging dread of uncertainty can leave us working scared.

This chapter can help both employees and leaders build a sense of stability and control – even when external conditions feel unstable. Though anyone may experience these feelings at work, the issues described in this chapter are particularly relevant for early-career employees and the suggested actions will be particularly useful for them.

Let's Look at Some Facts

- Job insecurity is a leading cause of stress: A recent study indicated that 54% of US workers report that job insecurity significantly increases their stress levels. The same report revealed that 75% of workers under the age of 26 report job insecurity as a major stressor.[1]

- Median US student loan debt exceeded $20,000 with 30% of all adults taking student loans for their education.[2] The financial burden shapes how younger workers experience stress at work during economic uncertainty.

- Financial stability is a key determinant of happiness and well-being. More than 80% of respondents in a recent study cited their long-term financial future and their day-to-day finances as factors contributing to their feeling of anxiety and stress.[3]

- Social media and peer comparisons often pressure younger workers to "look successful" even when they're financially stretched – often causing them to live beyond their means.

Leah's Story

Leah is a 25-year-old engineer working at a large, integrated energy company with operations around the world. The company recruited her shortly after she finished her master's degree in chemical engineering. She was excited by the opportunity. She had deep respect for the company and the industry. Just as important, the position alleviated some of her financial concerns. Leah had taken out substantial student loans to pay her way through undergraduate and graduate school. Landing the job felt like a breakthrough: a stable, well-paying position aligned with her values around energy transition and global impact.

But now, two years into the role, Leah has started to feel insecure. Oil prices are down. News reports speculate about a looming recession. To satisfy investors, the company has cancelled several large capital projects. There has been a hiring freeze. A colleague's contract wasn't renewed. In a recent town hall meeting, senior leaders spoke about "realigning priorities." No one used the word layoffs, but everyone interpreted the messages that way. This is an industry plagued by economic swings, and companies like hers react quickly to contain costs and stay competitive.

Leah's boss, Jeh, is a technically brilliant project leader with decades at the company. He's good-natured and a skilled leader who prioritizes his team. He juggles technical reviews, compliance briefings, and an endless stream of emails marked "urgent," all while trying to develop his employees. Leah is grateful to have such an empathetic manager. Even when under pressure, Jeh checks in regularly with Leah to see how she's doing. Despite Jeh's genuine outreach, Leah is reluctant to reveal how nervous she is caused by all the instability across the industry. Leah works late most nights, partly to prove herself and partly to reduce her fear of becoming redundant. But the extra effort isn't helping her sense of stability. She still wakes up in the middle of the night panicked. Her mind spins with questions: *What if I lose this job? What if I can't pay off my loans? What if I never feel secure enough to buy a house?*

She feels stuck between two truths: she wants to be loyal to a great company, and yet she knows loyalty doesn't guarantee anything anymore. Her friends talk openly about "keeping options open" and "quiet quitting," but that's not her style. She wants to stay and grow, but she also doesn't want to be caught off guard. Her uneasiness and restlessness are the tell-tales signs of working scared.

Eventually, her father offered a bit of wisdom from his own life lessons: "Stability isn't something the company gives you. It's something you build for yourself."

She took his advice to heart but wasn't sure what exactly to do to create a sense of stability amid all the economic turmoil.

Actions for Employees

In times of uncertainty, one of the most powerful things you can do is channel your energy into actions that help you stay grounded, prepared, and performing. While you can't control the economy or your company's decisions, you *can* shape how you approach your work, where you focus your energy, and how you broaden your capabilities. The following proven actions can help you do just that.

Focus on What You Can Control

In any situation, we can think of three categories to consider (Figure 7.1):

- What we can control
- What we can influence
- What we must accept as being beyond our control

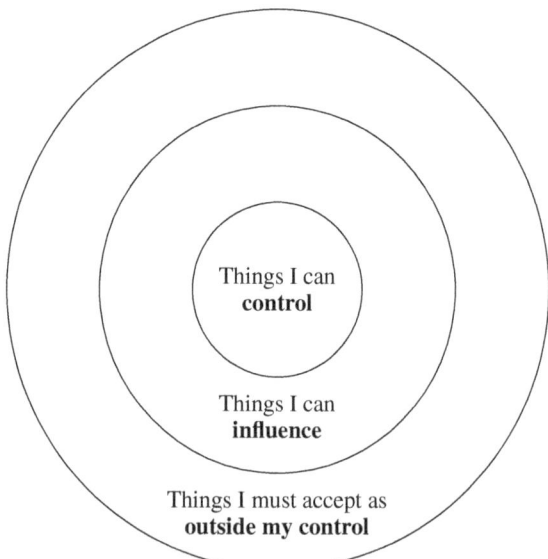

Figure 7.1 Zones of Control, Influence, and Acceptance

This model is commonly used in coaching, therapy, and leadership. It offers a powerful way to focus attention and energy.[4]

In the outermost circle are the things we must *accept as being outside our control*, such as economic shifts, policy decisions, or organizational changes. While it's natural to dwell on or complain about these events, our ability to alter them is limited.

The middle circle represents what we can *influence*. This may include advocating for a viewpoint, contributing to a project, or encouraging others to act. While we don't control the outcome, our efforts can help shape it. At the center of the circle is what we fully *control*.

This includes our attention, mindset, decisions, actions, and reactions. Filtering out the distractions of the outer ring while redirecting our attention toward the center serves to increase our impact while building competence, confidence, and calmness.

When you find yourself dwelling on a decision or problem, ask "what, if anything, can I change about this situation?"

In times of economic uncertainty, shift your attention from the dynamics outside your control toward your own habits, development, and contributions. You will be narrowing your focus on what lies within your control and influence. Remember you cannot control the economic environment, but you can control your preparation for and response to disruptive changes. Devoting your energy to these areas is time well spent. Here are a few specific areas to consider:

- **Build healthy habits.** Your personal habits are fully within your control. Develop a routine that strengthens your resilience and brings you joy. Creating predictability in your own routine can calm your nerves when the world outside feels frenetic. A helpful routine is one that includes small elements from your personal and professional life that help to ground you in a predictable rhythm.

Leah initially thought this strategy might be too simple to be much help. But she then recalled the advice from her father: stability is something you build for yourself. She started with small changes. A brisk walk with a neighbor before work each morning helped her to clear her mind. Before diving into work, she devoted time to clarifying her daily goals and priorities. In fact, she put a 15-minute placeholder on her schedule blocking the time each morning to ensure she would not be interrupted by competing meetings. During this time, she made a conscious and intentional commitment to the activities that would make the biggest impact for her, her team, and the organization. This step focused her energy on the important things within her control and pushed away those things that are beyond her influence.

- **Invest in your development.** Think of your professional development as a smart financial investment that starts paying off from day one. When you step outside your comfort zone to expand your skills, deepen your expertise, or broaden your perspective, you're not only making yourself more valuable to your organization and the market, but you are also strengthening your own sense of stability. In uncertain times, your enhanced capabilities can give you greater leverage, more options, and increased confidence in navigating change. The more you develop, the more secure you will feel, because your skills become assets no one can take away.

When Leah heard our advice to "invest in your development," she initially dismissed it. With budget cuts and hiring freezes in the air, it felt like survival was the priority, not professional growth. But then she realized something important: economic turmoil often creates opportunity. It is precisely when the economic landscape is shifting that there is a need to stand out; those who stay ahead of the curve will create a competitive advantage. Leah decided to grasp the opportunity – something she could do that is in her control. She volunteered for a cross-functional project that stretched her skill set. In addition, on her drive home from work, she listened to an audio course that described new trends and technologies in the energy sector. By building her worth, she felt she was taking more control of her destiny.

- **Dial up your contributions.** Oftentimes, no matter what is happening in the outside world, the best course of action is simply to continue to do your job as well as you can. Remember that excelling at everyday tasks will often distinguish you from the crowd. Meanwhile, focusing on your own contribution often brings a greater sense of control, confidence, and calm in a chaotic environment.

With her employer under increasing pressure, Leah knew that one thing she could control was how she showed up at work. She was good at her job and now more than ever, she needed to demonstrate that. She recommitted herself to her work. She reviewed process data for accuracy and made sure her documentation was consistently up to date. She applied some of her newfound knowledge to see opportunities others missed. She kept her internal stakeholders informed. Amidst the organizational chaos, Leah bolstered her reputation as a steady, reliable performer that her colleagues could depend on.

Figure Out Your Unique "Operating Manual"

We all respond to stress differently. One way to feel more secure during uncertain times is to understand how *you* operate – what helps you stay steady and what tends to throw you off course. When you know your patterns, you can make more intentional and successful choices about how to navigate challenges.

Here are five questions to help you create your personal "operating manual":

- What environments help me feel calm and competent? Be specific.
- When do I feel most focused and creative?
- What situations tend to spike my anxiety?
- When I've felt overwhelmed, what helped me calm down?
- What do I need to remind myself when I start to spiral into anxiety?

By reflecting on these questions ahead of time – when you're clear-headed – it will allow you to set yourself up for success. You can build your day around your natural strengths, do what you can to avoid the things or situations that trigger stress, and have a plan in place for when things go sideways. The more you understand your own patterns, the more secure you'll feel inside when the world outside feels unsteady.

We worked through these questions with Leah to help her better understand her "operating manual." As we explored her work situation and her typical responses, Leah realized that she is most creative and resilient early in the morning, and she needs a distraction-free environment to get the most challenging work done. In midafternoon, she recognized a dip in productivity. These are the times when she'd rather socialize with colleagues over a cup of coffee. These insights, combined with the freedom Jeh gave her to organize her own work, meant that Leah could organize her day according to her unique rhythm – one that played to her strengths and instilled confidence. During our discussions, Leah also admitted that she frequently woke up in the middle of the night feeling anxious about her job situation. As a remedy, she decided to put a notepad next to her bed to collect any nighttime worries, and then to revisit them in the morning with a clearer perspective. With fresh eyes, she started to see the patterns in her fears and could generate concrete tactics to alleviate them. Seeing the recurring patterns reminded her that she had successfully handled stress before. Doing this regularly brought an increasing sense of relief. Over time, Leah began to sleep through the night.

Track Your Value

Keep a log of small wins: things you learned, contributed, or improved. This can give you a sense of accomplishment and control. With time, this will become your internal scoreboard showing where and how you are winning.

The reality is that it's easy to lose track of what you've accomplished in the day-to-day rush. When it's time for a performance review, a discussion about a promotion, or considering an internal transfer, many people struggle to recall their contributions. Fortunately, this is an easy fix: find a simple way to capture your wins. Use a journal, a spreadsheet, a running email to yourself – whatever works – as long as you do it consistently.

This practice is consistent with the AIME Framework we introduced in Chapter 1. The M stands for Monitor and it's an essential part of progressing through a challenging situation. Keeping a current record of your accomplishments gives you something of value: evidence of your efforts, motivation to press on, and reassurance in times of need. Even if you never share it with anyone else, it's a quiet reminder that you're making progress, that your work matters, and that you are increasingly building your value. This will reinforce your sense of inner security even when the world outside feels uncertain. And if ever you do need to advocate for yourself, you'll be ready.

Practice Fiscal Responsibility

During times of economic uncertainty, fiscal responsibility is a powerful way of building your emotional stability. Each little bit of money saved will generate a greater sense of control and inner peace. In working with our clients, we remind them of two age-old strategies that have proven effective time and time again:

- **Stick to a budget – and revisit it often.** A budget can help you take care of yourself and your loved ones. We recommend thinking of your budget as a flexible framework, not a rigid constraint. It helps you make clear financial decisions when anxiety or outside pressure might otherwise cloud your judgment. As your circumstances change – whether it's a rent hike, a sudden expense, or an unexpected bonus – update your plan. Budgeting isn't a one-time exercise; it's an ongoing habit that builds your self-confidence, sense of control, and feelings of security.
- **Resist lifestyle creep.** When you get a raise or a job promotion, it is tempting to immediately level up your lifestyle – a nicer house, a new car, a vacation – after all, you've earned it. But if your lifestyle increases in lockstep with your pay increase, this leaves you just as vulnerable as before. Instead, we recommend trying to maintain your existing standard of living as long as possible. Use the extra income to build a cushion – save, invest, or pay down debt. That way, your professional progress builds your sense of security.

Leah's hard work paid off. In recognition of her efforts, her manager gave her an unexpected bonus. She treated herself to a dinner with friends to celebrate but resisted the urge to upgrade her lifestyle. Instead, she used the bulk of the bonus to pay down her student loans. It wasn't the flashy signal of accomplishment she might have liked, but it gave her a deeper sense of security and inner confidence – things that she considered priceless.

Expand Your Options by Building Flexibility

As the world feels more uncertain, build your flexibility. If you find ways to be more flexible, you will feel more prepared for and less trapped by dynamics outside your control. Flexibility can come from different sources: lifestyle, professional, financial, or mindset. Here are some questions to consider:

- Lifestyle:
  - Can I adjust my standard of living to bring a greater sense of stability?
  - Am I willing to relocate to reduce costs?
- Professional:
  - What new skills can I build?
  - What transferable skills do I have that I haven't fully leveraged?
  - Would I consider a lateral move?
  - Would I consider a remote or hybrid position to expand my professional options?
- Financial:
  - Can I reduce my expenses (even temporarily)?
  - Have I built a sufficient financial buffer that gives me room to maneuver?

- Mindset:
  - How can I adjust my definition of success? For example, can success for me include well-being, freedom, and/or development, not just compensation, productivity, or advancement?
  - How can I see opportunity even in the worst situation?

Leah found comfort in exploring these questions. As things at work grew more uncertain, she started thinking differently about what flexibility really meant. She didn't uproot her life, but she took stock of what *could* change if it had to. She decided she could move to a cheaper apartment, cut back on her spending for a while, or even take on a side project in another department to build her reputation. She also shifted her mindset by accepting the fact that a temporary setback would not derail her career. Finally, Leah reflected on her current notion of success. Sure, a promotion or raise would signal success; but that was not going to happen in these tough times. She decided to *expand* her definition of success. She would consider herself successful if she learned new skills, found joy in her work environment, and felt she was contributing to the global energy transition. Discovering she had some flexibility in her lifestyle, profession, finances, and even her mindset made a difference. Realizing where she still had room to maneuver gave her a reassuring sense of control.

**Building a Sense of Security in Uncertainty:
The Blueprint for Employees**

- Concentrate your energy on things within your control and influence
- Let go of the things you cannot control

- Figure out your "operating manual"
- Keep track of your successes and accomplishments
- Find ways to be a little more fiscally responsible
- Expand your options to bring greater flexibility into your current situation

Actions for Leaders

As we have emphasized throughout this book, leaders have a responsibility to care for their employees and to provide reassurance during turbulent times. We believe it is the hallmark of good leadership. The advice we offer can help you as a leader support your team through turmoil. Here are some practical actions that have proven to be effective:

Acknowledge Without Amplifying

Economic uncertainty often triggers fear – and fear is a persistent distraction. You may already sense that your employees are feeling stress from uncertainty. Ignoring that stress doesn't make it go away; it simply drives it underground. A more effective approach is to acknowledge the uncertainty without dramatizing it. Even a simple statement like, "I know this is a tough climate" helps employees acknowledge their own feelings and encourages them to manage their uneasiness, rather than letting it take over.

Leah's boss, Jeh, has done a good job of acknowledging the uncertainty. He makes it a practice of checking in with Leah to see how she is doing. At first, Leah found it hard to open up about her concerns, fearing that she might look weak. But Jeh acknowledged his own concerns about trends in the industry and rumors in the company. Just knowing that she was not alone helped Leah proactively manage, rather than ignore, the uneasiness she was feeling.

Share Your Practical Knowledge

Early-career employees benefit more from your tactical tips than simply reassurance. If you've weathered economic ups and downs in your own career, share how you coped. Your real-world stories such as "this is what helped me stay focused" or "here's how I built a safety net" can be invaluable lessons. Employees typically trust the opinions of their direct managers more than any other voice in an organization. Your employees will be receptive to your advice, especially if they know you've been through uncertainty yourself. Budgeting tips, personal routines, or even mindset shifts that helped you navigate tough times may seem basic to you now – but they can be invaluable to someone who's experiencing economic turmoil for the first time.

Introduce the Concept of "Stability Retrospectives"

When the present feels unsteady and the future feels scary, one of the most effective ways of gaining perspective is to look to the past. Reflecting on how you and your team have already navigated challenges can provide a sense of confidence that you can persevere through the current situation. With our clients, we use the process of Retrospective as a tool for learning in many situations. We have adapted this approach for use during times of economic instability or organizational uncertainty. We call them "Stability Retrospectives." These are short conversations that you can have with your employees to remind them that they've endured change in the past and persevered. You can use Stability Retrospectives in a team meeting or in one-on-one conversations. In either case, the approach is the same. We recommend you use the following simple questions to guide your employees through the discussion:

- "What stayed the same over the past 90 days?"
- "What changed – and what caused the change?"
- "What did you do that helped you handle those changes?"
- "What does that show you about how you can handle the next 90 days?"

Jeh used this technique in a one-on-one meeting with Leah. He noticed that she was rattled by some industry news that week that had been particularly grim. The uncertainty was starting to wear on her, affecting her focus and amplifying her concern about her future.

He told her to pause and look back over the previous 90 days. Here's how their conversation went as he asked her the questions, one-by-one:

- **What had stayed the same?** Her love of the company and the industry; her routines, both personal and professional; the respect she feels for her peers; the steady way that Jeh managed the team.
- **What had changed?** The cancelled capital projects would shift priorities for the team; some roles and responsibilities were being realigned around her; the mood in the team was more tense than before.
- **What had she done to manage it all?** She stayed focused on delivering good work; she offered to help a colleague adjust to the changes; she checked in with teammates more often; and she had started to practice her healthy habits.

As she talked it through, Leah started to see the situation with a new perspective. "I guess I've handled more than I realized," she said. That recognition, not a big breakthrough but a small shift, gave her a little more confidence to face whatever the next 90 days might bring.

Reinforce the Employee's Value

If you notice an employee struggling through the uncertainty, it is helpful to reiterate their value. You can't make the economic turmoil go away, but you can improve an employee's sense of security and self-esteem during that turmoil. When we feel recognized, we are more likely to feel emotionally secure. Dial up the message that their work is appreciated using the following approach:

- **Be specific.** Call out a clear example of what the employee did well. This makes it easier for them to understand, believe, and repeat the specific behavior.
- **Focus the feedback on something they can control.** Highlight actions or qualities that are within the employee's control. This helps them feel more grounded and capable during uncertain times.
- **Connect it to the team or bigger context.** Show how their contributions support the team's success. This reinforces a sense of belonging and helps them feel part of something meaningful. And it brings a greater sense of security.

Jeh does this regularly with his employees. For Leah, who is feeling insecure in the economic uncertainty, this kind of acknowledgment is especially impactful. In a recent one-on-one discussion with Leah, Jeh shared a specific observation that reinforced Leah's efforts:

> *"Leah, I've noticed how consistently you keep our stakeholders updated, like when you summarized the project changes in last Friday's email. That kind of clear, proactive communication is something you do really well, and it helps everyone stay aligned. Especially in turbulent times like this, it brings stability to the team and builds trust across the board. I really appreciate it."*

Notice that Jeh's observations highlight the things within Leah's and the team's control. This is an essential technique for gaining a greater sense of security.

Offer Structure and Focus

Remember that setting clear priorities is not only good management but also helps reduce employees' feelings of being overwhelmed. As a leader, you probably already offer structure and focus to your employees. In times of uncertainty, employees might get caught up in the turmoil and struggle to separate the urgent from the important. So, remember that reinforcing structure and giving focus during these situations not only keeps the work on track but can be a calming force in the storm. Help employees concentrate on what matters most now. This will increase their sense of control and confidence, which bolsters their sense of stability amid chaos.

Jeh did this for Leah without even realizing how helpful it was. During a particularly chaotic week, he pulled her aside and acknowledged that she might be getting mixed messages. He said, "For now,

I just want you to focus on the productivity improvement project we discussed yesterday. That's where we need your expertise the most. If you need me, let me know." It was a simple instruction, but for Leah, it felt like someone had quieted all the noise in the room. Instead of second-guessing where to spend her time, she had the direction she needed *and* the freedom to get it done. That structure and focus gave her a renewed sense of purpose in the middle of the storm.

> **Building a Sense of Security in Uncertainty: The Blueprint for Leaders**
>
> - Acknowledge the uncertainty through open conversation
> - Share your practical knowledge about persevering through uncertainty
> - Be a source of stability by role-modeling steadiness
> - Use "Stability Retrospectives" to learn from the past as you plan the present
> - Repeat, reinforce, and reiterate your employee's value
> - Emphasize structure and focus to help your team feel grounded

Chapter 8

Prioritizing Personal Well-Being

The ROI of Taking Care of Yourself

Do you feel relentless pressure to deliver? Are you exhausted by long hours? Do you have sudden mood changes? Do you struggle to get out of bed in the morning? These feelings might trigger fear – which means you might be working scared. All these symptoms relate to your feelings of personal well-being. Personal well-being includes one's physical, mental, and emotional states that affect employee productivity and job satisfaction. Your well-being and the well-being of your team is the focus of this chapter.

Let's Look at Some Facts

- According to the US Surgeon General, 76% of workers experienced at least one symptom of a mental health condition.[1]
- A global survey found one in four employees across demographics and from all over the world reported experiencing symptoms of burnout.[2]
- Stress levels are high, engagement is low with 40% of employees reporting stress and 21% reporting anger in a recent study. 62% of employees report being disengaged (i.e., quietly quitting), and 17% are *actively* disengaged (i.e., loudly quitting).[3]

- Employees report a steady decline in well-being: 50% report feeling stressed every day, 20% feel isolated, and 14% report a decline in their work-life balance since 2020.[4]
- Poor employee health erodes business performance. Depression and anxiety result in a loss of 12 billion working days per year, costing the global economy about $1 trillion annually.[5]

Howard's Story

Howard works in strategy and finance at a large international bank. He was hired about a year ago by his manager, Mike – someone he had worked with previously at a wealth management firm. Back then, Howard was a contract worker and considered Mike a great boss. They worked hard, but the pace felt manageable because they operated as a true team. However, when Mike brought Howard into the bank, it quickly became clear that Mike was under intense pressure. Mike had been tasked with integrating sourcing and procurement across 10 siloed divisions – a major organizational challenge. The pressure affected Mike's behavior. He was no longer the considerate leader Howard had once worked with. Instead, Mike began demanding unreasonable hours – late nights, weekends, even holidays.

Howard felt trapped. There was too much to do, and never enough time. One of Mike's non-negotiables was a mandatory daily 8:00 a.m. virtual meeting, which had become especially difficult for Howard to attend. Howard is a single father to his 12-year-old daughter, Cindy, who started at a new school this year. Her drop-off time conflicted directly with the meeting.

Howard explained to Mike that, as a divorced father with shared custody, he has Cindy half the time. On those mornings, he prepares her breakfast and drives her to school, something that is deeply important to him. He let Mike know that on the days he has Cindy, he wouldn't be able to attend the virtual meeting until 8:30, but that he'd be on time the rest of the week.

Unreasonable hours weren't unique to Mike's team. Howard noticed a broader cultural issue at the bank: employees were routinely expected to work weekends. Mike works every weekend – and he expects his team to follow suit. Making matters worse, Howard is working scared. He's heard rumors that his department may soon be reorganized. As a result, he feels pressure to put in extra hours to prove his value.

Eventually, Howard decided he needed to find a way to manage the overload. He approached Mike and asked, "Can you help me clarify my priorities?" Mike snapped, "Everything is a priority!" Howard also tried to set boundaries, but Mike insisted it was "very important" that Howard attend all meetings without exception.

This situation has left Howard physically and emotionally burned out. He feels constantly stressed. He no longer exercises or takes care of himself. He's working scared – afraid that if he doesn't do exactly what Mike wants, he'll lose his job.

This is an unhealthy situation – not just for Howard, but for the organization as well. As discussed earlier in this chapter, personal well-being is essential not only for individual health, but for overall productivity and performance. Let's now explore practical strategies that can help employees like Howard prioritize their personal well-being.

Actions for Employees

Define Your Boundaries

We all deserve the space to perform at our best – and the right to disconnect when the work is done. Taking time away from work to decompress and recover is essential for sustainable performance. Yet technology, constant connectivity, and unspoken expectations make "unplugging" increasingly difficult.

Many of our clients admit to saying "yes" to every work demand or responding at all hours. Not because they want to, but because they feel they have to. Over time, such crushing demands erode personal well-being and ultimately, job performance. To reclaim control and protect your well-being, start by defining three key types of boundaries. Each plays an essential role in helping you stay grounded:

- **Personal Boundaries (Work-Life Balance):** These boundaries protect the line between your work and personal time. Safeguarding private time ensures you can recharge, keep personal commitments, and ultimately preserve your long-term health and effectiveness.

- **Job Boundaries (Role and Responsibilities):** These boundaries clarify what falls within your job role – and what does not. Clear role boundaries help you manage expectations, prioritize effectively, and avoid overcommitting to tasks that rightfully belong to someone else.

- **Interpersonal Boundaries (Respect and Behavior):** These boundaries define how you expect to be treated. They clarify what is acceptable in terms of communication and behavior. They help you perform at your best, while also preserving psychological safety and ensuring mutual respect.

Articulate and Tactfully Defend Your Boundaries

Once you have defined your boundaries for yourself, the next step is to articulate them to others. Most importantly, share them with your manager. Reinforce your boundaries with tact and consistency. These are important conditions worth defending, but you do not want to seem rigid or confrontational. Instead, it is about being clear, respectful, confident, and self-aware.

Here's a simple 4-step approach we've successfully taught our clients to use with their teams:

1. **Clarify what you need** regarding your personal life, job responsibilities, and how you expect to be treated.
2. **Be direct, but respectful** when expressing your boundaries. Tact builds trust and preserves the relationship.
3. **Don't apologize** for honoring your needs. Setting boundaries is a sign of your strength, not a weakness.
4. **Express appreciation** when others respond with understanding and support. Your positive response will reinforce the behavior you want to see.

Howard realized he couldn't attend every 8:00 a.m. meeting on time due to his morning responsibilities with his daughter. Instead of silently resenting the situation or overextending himself, he set up time to meet with his manager, Mike. During their meeting, Howard acknowledged the importance of the meetings but explained why his morning commitment to his daughter Cindy was equally important. He held firm. He calmly described the situation and the emotional burden it carried. Mike was initially silent, but then said he understood the difficulty of the situation. Howard's willingness to explain, not to justify, his position helped build trust. He also expressed gratitude for Mike's willingness to listen and adjust his expectations. During the meeting, they agreed to try a new approach and to revisit it later if they needed to adjust the approach. The balance of Howard's clarity, tact, and flexibility made the conversation constructive and led to a desired outcome.

Respect the Boundaries of Others to Reinforce a Healthy Team Culture

Chances are, your colleagues have boundaries of their own, some clearly stated and others more subtle or unspoken. Encourage them to share with you what they need and show that you respect their preferences. By demonstrating that you understand and honor their boundaries, you make it more likely they will respect yours in return. When mutual boundary-setting becomes part of everyday interaction, it fosters healthier interactions and improves overall well-being across the team.

Build Your "Wellness Network" as a Means of Support

Research shows that personal well-being is directly correlated to the quality of support we receive from others. That's why we encourage you to build what we call your "Wellness Network." This encompasses a group of trusted individuals who can support you emotionally, offer practical advice, and help you keep your wellness top of mind. This network can include both personal and professional relationships – peers, confidantes, mentors, and coaches – each offering a different kind of support.

Peers

Talking with peers who are facing similar challenges can provide relief, validation, and a sense of connection. It helps to know you're not alone. That said, it's important to be mindful: spending too much time commiserating with others can unintentionally reinforce negativity. Look for peers who not only empathize with your situation but also offer constructive insights and emotional balance. For example, Howard had a peer in London named Lawrence who held the same role at the bank. Although they had never met in person, Lawrence quickly picked up on the fact that Howard was overwhelmed. It helped Howard to hear that Lawrence, too, was "working scared" due to similar pressure – and to learn how he was managing it. Lawrence's empathy, insight, and practical suggestions helped Howard feel less isolated and improved his overall well-being.

Confidantes

Confidantes are those people in your life with whom you can be completely yourself. They allow you to be vulnerable without judgment and offer support when you need it most. Howard leaned on a close friend who was also a family member to talk through the stress he was experiencing at work. Their willingness to listen, along with their valuable advice, made a meaningful difference. Take some time to identify the friends or relatives in your life who can serve this role – people whom you can rely on to have your best interests at heart.

Mentors

Mentors offer another powerful form of support. These are experienced professionals, often within your organization, who can provide camaraderie, guidance on career decisions, or help tackle a difficult issue you may be facing. For Howard, he found a mentor in Mary, the Manager of Strategy and Finance, because he admired her leadership values and the way she juggled work and family life. Mary agreed to meet for weekly lunches, providing both support and insight. Mentors like Mary can be vital sources of stability in high-pressure work environments.

Coaches

Coaches are external professionals who can provide structured, impartial support to help you navigate challenges and support your growth. As executive coaches, we've worked with individuals like Howard to help them stay aligned with their organization's goals while also safeguarding their mental and emotional well-being. Many of the actions in this chapter – and in the prior chapters – are drawn directly from these real-world coaching engagements. When you build a strong connection with a coach, the sessions can help you gain clarity, increase adaptability, and move toward sustainable success – not at the cost of your well-being, but by strengthening it.

Develop an Exit Strategy, Just in Case

If you're in a work environment that's unlikely to improve, one option to consider is leaving your role. But, even if you decide to stay, we believe thinking through your exit strategy can be a valuable coping tool. It may simply be time for you to do the next thing. Perhaps you've tried everything, yet your well-being continues to suffer. Are there other roles within your organization that might be a better fit? Or is it time to explore external opportunities? If so, be sure your résumé and online profiles are polished, up to date, and highlight your unique strengths. As you work to improve your current environment, knowing that you're prepared to leave, if necessary, can help you increase your well-being – no matter what comes next.

> **Prioritizing Personal Well-Being:
> The Blueprint for Employees**
>
> - Define your boundaries clearly
> - Maintain your boundaries
> - Respect the boundaries of others
> - Build your "Wellness Network"
> - Develop an exit strategy

Actions for Leaders

Remember that as a team leader in a large organization, you may not be able to control everything at the company level – but you do have tremendous influence within your own team. You play a central role in shaping the day-to-day experience of your people, which is the true source of work culture. Use your influence to foster a team culture that prioritizes and protects employee well-being. When you safeguard well-being, you create the foundation for sustainable performance. This is the true return-on-investment (ROI) of well-being – not just feeling better but *performing* better over time. The most effective workplace well-being strategies are not found in apps or company wellness programs; they're found in your leadership behaviors. How you manage workload, mitigate stress, communicate authentically, and delegate thoughtfully will define the health of your team.[6,7,8] You, as a leader, set the tone. With that in mind, let's explore techniques we have used to help leaders create a healthier environment, support employee well-being, and maintain performance.

Discuss Healthy Boundaries and Respect Those Boundaries

Have a dedicated conversation with your employees about boundaries. Ask what matters most to them – and share what matters to you. You'll likely find common ground that supports both well-being and team performance. Examples of respectful leadership behavior include acknowledging and safeguarding employees' personal time, as well as communicating preferences and job responsibilities. Respecting personal time is essential. For instance, when assigning deliverables, be intentional about setting realistic deadlines that don't encroach on employees' time off. Emergencies may arise occasionally, but when they do, be clear in your communication that these are exceptions – not a reflection of your general leadership style.

Employees may also differ in how they prefer to receive feedback. Some may appreciate direct input in a private setting, while others may be comfortable discussing boundaries in a group. Whenever possible, accommodate these preferences.

Check-In Regularly to See How Your Employees Are Feeling

Most good leaders check in to see how their employees are *doing*. We want to encourage you to check in to see how your employees are *feeling*. This opens the conversation about well-being. We suggest to clients that they ask three short questions that highlight what's working and what can be improved, such as:

- What's one thing we're doing well, as an organization, to create a healthy environment for you?
- What's one thing we could improve, as an organization, to increase your feeling of well-being?

- What's something that I, as your manager, could do to help increase your well-being?

When leaders act on the answers to these three questions – even small improvements – they are demonstrating a commitment to employee health, and they are on their way to building a culture that promotes employee wellness.

Watch for Warning Signs of Poor Well-Being

You might see an employee who is burned out, stressed, depressed, or lacks motivation. Heed these early warning signs; don't wait to open dialogue. Meet privately to surface the issues and diagnose the causes. It might be caused by factors outside the organization (e.g., new competition in the industry), factors inside the organization (e.g., organizational changes), your leadership style (e.g., lack of feedback), and/or the employee (e.g., family issues, financial problems). Whatever the cause, speaking about any of these factors is likely to provide some relief. And, even if the cause is outside your control, you may have some options to mitigate the effects. Mike failed to do any of this with Howard even though he noticed the signs of poor well-being. If Mike had intervened with his employee, he would have learned that Howard feels overwhelmed and time constrained. Mike would have discovered that Howard is working scared, and it's impacting his health and performance.

Help Employees Prioritize Their Activities

Like Howard, many employees feel that they have too much to do, and not enough time to do it. Many employees think all tasks need to get done – right now. The truth is that some tasks are more important than others. You can increase your employees' feeling of personal well-being by helping them prioritize their activities. A method we use with our clients is a Prioritization Matrix, also known as the "Eisenhower Matrix."[9] It differentiates tasks based on urgency and importance, offering you and your employees a useful technique to categorize, prioritize, and discuss activities. Look at Figure 8.1.

Activities that are *important and urgent* are those you should DO NOW. These are things you deem to be high-value, time-sensitive activities requiring your attention and contribution. Examples include addressing a crisis, delivering on a customer need, or meeting an urgent deadline. Items that are *important, but not urgent* fall into the PLAN quadrant. These are high-value tasks that are not time-sensitive. Examples include long-term planning or relationship building. For activities that you consider *urgent, but not important,*

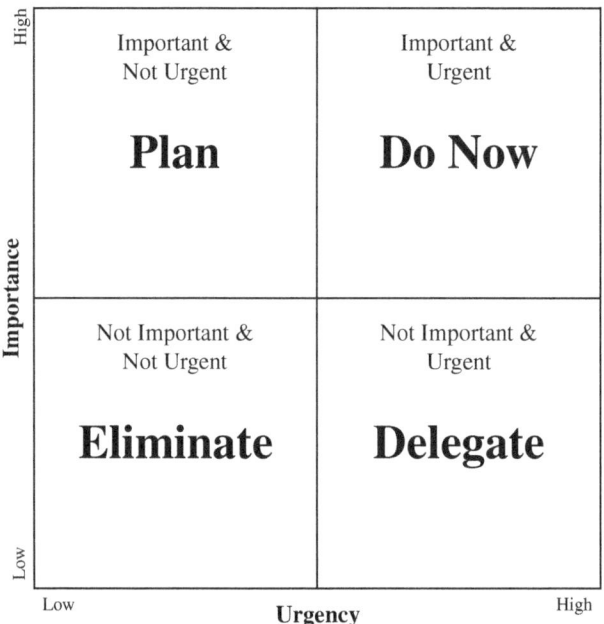

Figure 8.1 Prioritization Matrix to Categorize Actions by Importance and Urgency

you should DELEGATE to others. These are tasks that need to get done but do not necessarily require your expertise or attention. This could be asking one of your employees to attend a weekly meeting in your place. Finally, you may discover some tasks are *neither important nor urgent*. You should ELIMINATE these tasks since they are low-value distractions. An example is attending a standing meeting where nothing gets accomplished.

Recall what Mike said to Howard when Howard asked what his priorities should be. What Mike said makes no sense. If everything is a priority, *then nothing is a priority*!

Direct Employees to Wellness Resources

At the beginning of the chapter, we said that corporate well-being programs or self-help tools are not enough. Nothing can replace your good leadership. But these programs and tools do offer valuable support that can complement the other recommendations in this chapter. Therefore, direct your team members to appropriate wellness programs that your organization offers. Most companies offer some tools, such as physical health programs, mental health support, and work-life balance programs to employees. They can provide an additional means of support to help maintain employee well-being. For instance, we endorse stress management programs that encourage employees to use the stress reduction techniques that we discussed in Chapter 6.

Model Healthy Behaviors and Speak Openly About Personal Well-Being

Always remember: your team is observing your behavior, whether you realize it or not. That's why it's essential to role model the behaviors you want to see, especially when it comes to building a healthy team culture.

A client of ours shared a compelling example. A senior manager explained that he was planning to leave the office at 3:00 p.m. to catch a flight for his upcoming vacation. He could have quietly slipped out of the office. Instead, he made it a point to say out loud that he was leaving. He wanted to send the message to his team that it is okay to have a personal life. He intentionally wanted to transmit the message that taking vacations is expected. Time off should not be short-changed – yet many employees in today's workplace feel pressure to do so.[10]

The opposite is also true: when leaders model unhealthy behaviors, the damage spreads. For example, Howard's manager, Mike, boasted about working every weekend as a sign of commitment. Predictably, his team then mirrored his behavior. The result was a harmful cycle that fueled burnout, eroded well-being, and ultimately diminished team performance.

As a leader, your actions carry more weight than your words. Use them wisely.

**Prioritizing Personal Well-Being:
The Blueprint for Leaders**

- Discuss boundaries – theirs and yours
- Check-in regularly
- Watch for warning signs
- Offer guidance on priorities
- Provide resources
- Model healthy behaviors

Bringing It All Together

The Toolbox to Succeed During Turbulent Times

We wrote this book because we believe there are practical steps people can take to succeed in turbulent times. In the preceding pages, we presented **more than 100 actions** designed to help you navigate the turbulent scenarios described in each chapter. Looking across these many recommendations, common themes emerge – what we call the **10 Keys for Success**. In our consulting work, we have consistently found these 10 capabilities to be essential for every effective employee. They are therefore worth cultivating and strengthening.

By learning and applying the actions in this book, you will strengthen your effectiveness in the **10 Keys for Success**. These actions will not only help you cope with your *specific* turbulent situation but will also make you a more valuable contributor to your organization in *any* context. For example, even if your company is not undergoing a merger or acquisition, the Actions for Employees and Leaders in Chapter 6 can still strengthen your skills, enhance your performance, and support your long-term career success.

The 10 Keys for Success

The 10 Keys for Success are life skills that you can continue to build and refine throughout your career. Whether you are new to the workforce, a mid-level manager, or a senior executive, improving incrementally in each of these Keys will increase your value and enhance your job satisfaction. In this way, you can consider the turbulent situations in the book, though difficult, as opportunities to learn and grow in these 10 Keys for Success.

Key 1: Deepen Self-Awareness

Your success requires you to understand yourself and articulate your traits to others. Everyone has unique experiences, preferences, values, and motivators. Self-aware individuals know what drives them; thus they are better equipped to navigate turbulence.

Key 2: Enhance Self-Management

Your effectiveness depends on your ability to manage your time, actions, and emotions. Successful employees can proactively clarify expectations with their manager, focus on what they can control, regulate their feelings, turn fear into action, and prioritize their well-being.

Key 3: Develop a Positive Mindset

Positive thinking is a powerful game changer for emotional, physical, and mental health. Replace your negative self-talk with positive messages and highlight the good aspects of your work. Sharing the positives of work with colleagues while downplaying negatives can boost everyone's job satisfaction.

Key 4: Take Ownership

Many things in the workplace are outside your control, but that doesn't mean you should sit idly by. Don't be a victim. Whatever the situation, there are many things that are within your control – from handling your reaction, to deciding on your response, to managing your career choices. When employees focus their energies on the things they can influence, they use their energy and effort most effectively.

Key 5: Build Learning Agility

As the demands of work change, so too must your skills and capabilities. Employees and managers alike should commit to lifelong learning – expanding their capabilities, building new skills, acquiring new knowledge, and embracing new opportunities.

Key 6: Exercise Adaptability

Some changes are welcome, others are difficult, but one thing is for certain – change is inevitable in today's organizations. To succeed, you not only need to adapt to change, you should champion it. The key to adaptability is aiming for a meaningful goal and adapting behavior – step-by-step – to stay aligned with that goal.

Key 7: Communicate Authentically

Success depends heavily on the ability to articulate your thoughts, feelings, and requirements clearly. Communication is essential for seeking feedback on performance, voicing thoughts in meetings, articulating unique value, and safeguarding boundaries.

Key 8: Leverage Healthy Relationships

No one succeeds alone. When you actively strengthen relationships and intentionally expand your network, you increase your visibility, value, and contribution. Building and maintaining healthy connections helps to stay informed, supported, and engaged.

Key 9: Cultivate Teamwork

More than ever, your work is accomplished in team settings. Hybrid work environments test these interactions even further. When teams are dispersed, strong relationships help members feel connected to one another and committed to shared goals.

Key 10: Improve Continuously

Whatever you are doing today, you can do a little better tomorrow. You can be more effective – and make your organization more successful – when you continually and patiently refine how you work and contribute. Small incremental improvements over time add up to major progress.

Matrix and the Toolbox

The turbulent situations described in this book create distinct opportunities to develop your **10 Keys for Success**. The matrix below illustrates the links between the chapter topics and the Keys. These links indicate how the actions from each chapter enhance your key skills in these critically important areas.

Matrix 10.1 Important links between the chapter topics and the 10 Keys for Success

	Key 1 Self-Awareness	Key 2 Self-Management	Key 3 Positive Mindset	Key 4 Ownership	Key 5 Learning Agility	Key 6 Adaptability	Key 7 Communication	Key 8 Relationship-Building	Key 9 Teamwork	Key 10 Continuous Improvement
Chapter 1: Adapting to a Changing Workplace	☑	☑	☑	☑	☑	☑				☑
Chapter 2: Succeeding Amidst Arrogant Leadership	☑	☑		☑	☑	☑	☑	☑		☑
Chapter 3: Amplifying Your Voice in a Team Culture		☑		☑			☑	☑	☑	☑
Chapter 4: Thriving in a Hybrid Team	☑	☑			☑		☑	☑	☑	

(continued)

	Key 1 Self-Awareness	Key 2 Self-Management	Key 3 Positive Mindset	Key 4 Ownership	Key 5 Learning Agility	Key 6 Adaptability	Key 7 Communication	Key 8 Relationship-Building	Key 9 Teamwork	Key 10 Continuous Improvement
Chapter 5 Enduring a Restructuring/Downsizing	☑	☑	☑	☑		☑		☑	☑	☑
Chapter 6: Prevailing Through Mergers and Acquisitions			☑		☑	☑	☑		☑	☑
Chapter 7: Building a Sense of Security Amidst Economic Turmoil	☑		☑	☑		☑				☑
Chapter 8: Prioritizing Personal Well-Being	√	☑	☑	☑	☑	☑		☑	☑	√

Think of the actions in each chapter as a **Toolbox** that you can use both to navigate turbulent situations and to steadily strengthen your skills in the workplace. As a handy reference, the following **Toolbox** reiterates the 100+ actions and describes how they help you build your skills in the **10 Keys for Success**.

Toolbox: Summary of Employee and Leader Actions

Chapter 1: Adapting To a Changing Workplace
Actions for Employees

- **Acknowledge the emotions that change triggers.** Pause to understand and accept your emotions. This builds greater self-awareness and helps you manage reactions constructively. By staying honest with yourself, you create steadiness even in uncertain times. Describe the feeling in your own words before deciding on the next step to take.

- **Use the AIME Model for Change to guide your efforts toward a meaningful goal.** Use our framework to take steady, intentional steps so that change feels more like a *choice*. AIME stands for *Align, Integrate, Monitor,* and *Elevate*. Start small to gain momentum – choose one goal, practice one new behavior, or monitor a single step in progress before expanding your efforts. Using this framework increases your sense of ownership and promotes adaptability by highlighting how to aim toward a meaningful goal, reinforcing the behavior that gets you there, and tracking progress along the way.

    - **A = ALIGN your efforts toward *your* goal.** Define what matters most to you to clarify your direction and deepen your self-awareness. Write your goal down and keep it visible as a reminder of where to focus. Set an intention to fuel a positive mindset, because you know what you're working toward and why it matters.

- **I = INTEGRATE productive thoughts and behaviors.** Practicing new behaviors until they become second nature builds continuous improvement. Ask yourself, "Is this behavior moving me closer to my goal or further way?" This increase in self-awareness will help you make conscious choices that keep you moving in the desired direction.

- **M = MONITOR and acknowledge progress.** Pay attention to both small and large signs of growth to reinforce learning agility, since you're building on what works and adjusting based on your observations and feedback from others. Keep a log of what went well, what was hard, and what you'd do differently – this turns progress into greater insight. It also deepens self-awareness, as you notice patterns in what helps or hinders your success.

- **E = ELEVATE efforts to build on success.** Leverage your progress to expand your efforts. This boosts a positive mindset and generates momentum. After noticing a success – even a small one – ask yourself: "How can I build on this?" For example, after successfully completing a small project, an employee decides to lead a larger initiative or coordinate with another team on a project. Expanding on what is working demonstrates learning agility and builds ownership for ambitious goals.

- **Revisit the AIME Model regularly to stay on track.** Use the framework throughout the change journey. Use it as a reminder of the goal you want to achieve and to guide the steps you take along the way, especially when the path gets rocky.

Actions for Leaders

- **Create space to process.** Encourage employees to share what change means to them – including both supportive and critical sentiments. Create dedicated time in team meetings and in one-on-one discussions for employees to share their thoughts and feelings about the change. This practice develops self-awareness and deepens your relationships with your employees. While it may feel like slowing down, this often generates speed and sustained momentum for change.

- **Explain and reiterate the rationale.** Provide clear and consistent explanations to reduce uncertainty and to help your employees focus on the bigger picture. Use clear language and repeat the key points across multiple forums (e.g., emails, meetings, conversations) so employees hear a consistent message. Doing so strengthens adaptability and reinforces a positive mindset across the team.

- **Apply the AIME Model for Change to guide and support.** Use the model in your coaching conversations to provide a clear framework to support your employees. AIME helps *Align* your efforts with clear goals, *Integrate* new behaviors into daily practice, *Monitor* progress through visible signs of growth, and *Elevate* performance by reinforcing what works. In coaching conversations, walk employees through the AIME steps and encourage each person to apply one step immediately, then follow up to reinforce progress. As you work through the model over successive conversations, you will reinforce your employees' ownership for taking on bigger tasks. As your team steps up, this will expand your capacity as a leader.

- **Treat adaptability as a skill set – and train your team to change.** Treat changeability like any other job skill – define, develop, measure, and reinforce it. Ask about past change experiences. Include adaptability goals in development plans and performance reviews. Offer stretch projects that build change capacity, and offer coaching, feedback, and recognition. When you build change readiness into your everyday leadership practices, you develop your team's change skills and help them perform through turbulent times.

- **Foster psychological safety.** Create an environment where employees feel comfortable sharing concerns, asking questions, and experimenting with new approaches. Make sure they feel safe to take smart risks, ask for help, or admit a mistake. Respond to mistakes supportively rather than with blame to encourage smart risk-taking and learning. When people know they will not be judged or punished for speaking up, they are far more willing to engage fully and embrace meaningful change.

- **Be a consistent and stabilizing force.** Align what you do with what you have said. When you model integrity, your employees know what you expect and that you will apply the rules fairly. Follow through on commitments, hold yourself to the same standards as your team, and address any inconsistencies quickly. This consistency builds teamwork and collaboration, while creating a stable environment where experimentation and learning can flourish.

- **Communicate transparently.** Share honest updates, even when the news is uncertain or negative to reduce speculation and increase clarity. Offer regular updates, use multiple channels, and deliver difficult messages clearly and with empathy. Share your own uncertainties. Authentic leadership builds connection and trust.

- **Use micro-Performance Indicators (mPIs) to acknowledge and celebrate small steps in progress.** Highlight everyday progress by introducing the concept of micro-Performance Indicators (mPIs). An mPI is a small, but meaningful change that contributes to a new habit, interaction, or a greater goal. Use mPIs to complement KPIs to get a broader sense of progress – capturing large-scale, quantitative metrics with KPIs while acknowledging the many small, qualitative improvements through mPIs. Recognizing these little moments nurtures a positive mindset and fuels continuous improvement, keeping employees motivated to grow steadily.

Chapter 2: Succeeding Amidst Arrogant Leadership

Actions for Employees

- **Strengthen your position in the organization.** Consider that no matter how well you think you are performing in your present job, what could possibly happen if your performance improved? There is no penalty for continuous improvement and becoming better. Seek out developmental opportunities and gain new skills.

- **Understand why your manager may exhibit arrogant behaviors.** Acknowledge your manager's point of view. Knowing that an arrogant manager may have low self-esteem, recognize those areas where you agree or you think they have a good idea. When they have a good idea, recognize it and let them know you appreciate it.

- **Focus on key responsibilities and performance expectations/deliverables.** Clarify with your manager, recognizing that they have many additional direct reports. Enhance your self-management by monitoring your own performance each month and comparing your current level of performance with your performance expectations. By accomplishing them, you are not only making yourself more successful, but also your manager and the organization more successful.

- **Document your contributions.** Remember that successful performance in most jobs is a combination of effective behaviors and achieved results. It is critical that you document when you successfully achieve significant performance improvements regarding your behavior and results on each of your key responsibilities. Through effective self-management, you can effectively discuss any discrepancies in performance between your perspective and your manager's perspective.

- **Seek feedback from those in your orbit.** Ask, "What is one thing I could do differently to be more effective?" When you receive regular feedback from managers, colleagues, and clients, it allows you to continually learn as you progress in your role. The more self-awareness you have, the better equipped you are to navigate through difficult times and set yourself up for success.

- **Expand how you seek feedback.** Recall that employees who have more *arrogant* leaders rate their feedback environment less favorably. If you ask your boss for *advice*, they will be more likely to think forward to future opportunities to improve rather than backward to the things you have done, which you can no longer change. When asking for advice, ask how a situation should be handled and how these kinds of situations should be handled in the future. In this way, you are playing to your boss's ego by asking for advice and becoming more future oriented, thereby allowing yourself to continually improve. This is a good tactic both for managing an arrogant boss and for improving your performance – a win-win situation.

Actions for Leaders

- **Become an enlightened leader through feedback.** Feedback can help you gain some self-awareness and ensure you are perceived as confident, not arrogant. Acknowledge and credit others' ideas during meetings. Make sure your personal agenda is not above that of the organization. Ask for and accept constructive feedback and take responsibility for your own mistakes. When receiving negative feedback, ask for ways that you could handle a particular situation more effectively. And finally, create an environment where your staff tells you what you need to hear, *not* what you want to hear!

- **Create a culture of feedback through a 360° process.** Participate in a thorough feedback process to obtain feedback from multiple sources, including your manager, direct reports, and peers. They will provide insight into your level of effectiveness on numerous leadership attributes. Share your report with your manager as well as your direct reports. By making the results public, you will be more committed to making effective changes.

- **Communicate your willingness to change.** Be clear in your communication with your staff. For example, let your direct reports know you take the feedback from the 360° feedback survey seriously, and to show your adaptability, next year you will participate again with the goal that your direct reports will see the positive changes that will occur in your behavior.

- **Collaborate for role clarity.** Sit down with your direct reports individually to clarify key responsibilities and performance expectations. This will allow for the feedback you give to be more productive and supportive of their development efforts.

Commit to tying your feedback, both positive and negative, back to their key responsibilities and performance expectations. Few employees can maintain high levels of motivation without effective feedback.

- **Ensure that the feedback you give to employees is appropriate.** Reflect on the feedback you want to give by asking yourself, "Does the feedback fit the employee?", "Will it be meaningful enough to help the employee improve?", "Is the feedback specific and directly related to employee job performance?" Finally, make sure to communicate how the feedback helps the employee, the department, and the organization overall.

Chapter 3: Finding Your Voice in a Team Culture

Actions for Employees

- **Observe and listen to collect data.** Observe before speaking so you can see patterns and understand team dynamics more clearly. Note who speaks most, who tends to stay quiet, or how decisions get made before joining the discussion. This discipline builds self-awareness and self-management, and it helps you contribute to stronger teamwork.

- **Build your confident voice, step-by-step by starting with easier messages.** Begin with smaller contributions and work toward higher-stakes messages to grow your confidence gradually. Practice by preparing a short point or question before each meeting and then committing yourself to share it. This approach strengthens your communication skills in how you express yourself.

- **Use the 5W Framework to prepare for high-stakes messages.** Prepare your message by considering "Who, What, Where, When, and Why" so your ideas are clear and structured, and tailored to the situation and need. Draft your key message in advance and quickly run through the 5Ws to see if anything important is missing. Doing so sharpens your communication skills and increases your adaptability across different contexts.

- **Test your messages with safe peers to build your confidence.** Share your thoughts with trusted colleagues in low-risk settings to gain feedback and build confidence. Run your point by a peer or in a quick chat before you bring it up in a full team meeting. This approach enhances your trusted relationships and strengthens your learning agility before speaking in larger forums.

- **Frame your comments to open up the dialogue.** Phrase your contributions in ways that encourage discussion rather than stifling it. Phrasing as a question or suggestion rather than a critique will promote teamwork and build more effective teamwork within your group. For example, try starting with "what if we tried. . ." or "how would it work if. . ." to spur conversation.

- **Strengthen your voice through regular practice – and help others find their voice.** Practice speaking often so it becomes easier and more natural – and so you create space for others to do the same. Begin by commenting on low-risk topics, then gradually move to more complex issues as your confidence builds. This increases your ability to take ownership for ideas, activities, and outcomes. It also results in continuous improvement in your team interactions.

Actions for Leaders

- **Change the "risk-reward calculus" of speaking up to make the risk worthwhile.** Reduce the perceived risks of contributing and increase the rewards. Doing so gives employees a greater willingness to speak. Even if a suggestion isn't adopted, acknowledge the effort of an honest attempt. Thank employees or highlight how their input contributed to the discussion. This will spur their sense of ownership and motivate them to communicate more openly, lifting the overall quality of team interactions.

- **Invite all the voices – early and often – to encourage contribution.** Get input from a wide range of perspectives to ensure every voice is heard. In team meetings, begin with input from each team member (e.g., a quick check-in, a question, a thought to share). Consider rotating who opens discussions or explain that you will call on each person one-by-one. In this way, even quieter voices get heard consistently. When everyone speaks early, they are more likely to stay engaged. This practice reinforces the kind of teamwork and shared accountability that leads to sustained performance.

- **Manage your reaction.** Remember that actions speak louder than words. If you want to create a culture where people speak up, you must ensure your reactions to contributions – especially unexpected ones – reinforce speaking up rather than shutting it down. Doing this well will deepen your self-management, especially in times of stress.

- **Set and follow your team's "interaction principles."** Establish clear expectations for how the team engages, collaborates, and makes decisions. Then role model it yourself. Consider formalizing the principles in a team charter or revisiting these principles at the start of major projects to keep them top-of-mind. Doing so strengthens teamwork and supports individual self-management, giving everyone clarity in how to interact productively.

- **Provide development opportunities.** Offer various paths for your employees to stretch and develop to build their learning agility. This includes training and development opportunities or taking on new tasks and roles within the team. Create opportunities such as pairing less experienced employees with mentors or rotating responsibilities to expand exposure. As your team learns new skills, it will also deepen their self-awareness as they discover their individual strengths and growth areas.

Chapter 4: Thriving in a Hybrid Team

Actions for Employees

- **Advocate through tracking toward your goals.** Create good methods of tracking the work you are doing, record any questions you have throughout the week, and create a good agenda for any 1:1 meetings with your manager. You can enhance your communication skills and provide more visibility into your work that your manager may not have known about. The more you can advocate for yourself, and take control of your narrative, the more likely you are to earn a promotion or be considered for leadership.

- **Seek support.** Ask for advice or support if you feel like you are on an island. Be transparent with your manager, ask for advice and share your feelings when needed. This can help to improve communication between yourself and your manager.

- **Build in-office relationships.** Use your in-office days to meet with your manager and have more informal conversations than you would when you are working remotely. When possible, spend time with your peers and co-workers to build more effective relationships. Go to lunch or arrange a team event after work to get to know one another better. These things will help you build more trust with your colleagues. Focus on developing meaningful relationships with team members during your time together. Use lunch and break time as an opportunity to build relationships and learn about what's "really" happening in and around the business. Many insights come from unplanned interactions and informal discussions.

- **Focus on establishing effective relationships with your peers and cross-functional teams.** Pay particular attention to cross-functional tasks. Spend time on building a stronger personal relationship with these team members. They will be more motivated and accomplish more on the cross-functional projects they are working on. Effective team players show more interest in the success of their team than in being proved "right." They're willing to listen to opposing viewpoints, if the ideas are in the best interest of their team.

- **Segment your time.** Allocate time to set yourself up for success because it is important to segment your efforts by your work environment. For many, work requiring deep concentration is better when working from home. On the other hand, developing relationships, cross-functional alignment efforts, brainstorming activities, group work sessions, etc. are all better for the in-office work environment.

- **Leverage technology to promote communication.** Use collaboration platforms such as Slack and Teams Messaging as a way of increasing your informal interactions. By learning and using these available software tools efficiently, it can increase quick team interactions, replicating some of the benefits of being on-site together, and enhances communication.

Actions for Leaders

- **Build trust through one-on-ones.** Ask questions and encourage your direct reports to share their accomplishments and challenges. Make sure you are taking time to include personal discussions and talk about life outside of work to help foster a good relationship built on trust.

- **Maximize in-person team meetings.** Have a clear agenda for the team meeting to help foster good teamwork and build collaborative relationships. When setting up an agenda, prioritize talking points. As the meeting leader, you are uniquely positioned to promote a positive meeting environment. Your mood as the meeting leader is a good predictor of the eventual mood of the attendees.

- **Provide support through change.** Know your team and know who might be most affected by a return-to-office policy. Many employees have grown to love the hybrid environment, while others struggle. Provide your team members with adequate support to adapt to the work environment. Listen carefully as to what you can bring up to senior leadership that your team has concerns about. Just knowing you will do your best to advocate for your employees, whether it works or not, often goes a long way toward building collaborative relationships.

- **Clarify team norms.** Collaborate with your team to come up with agreements on such things as response times to emails and informal use of technology. Make sure that the team members have access and training regarding these technologies, when necessary. This will enhance communication among your team members.

- **Use anchor days to enhance collaboration.** Establish "anchor days" for hybrid workforces in line with departmental needs. Remember that they are only worthwhile if everyone from your team can be there. Therefore, when possible, attendance should be mandatory. This can help provide for better and more effective teamwork.

- **Look for additional ways to enhance employee appreciation.** Show your gratitude to employees from time to time and make your appreciation genuine so it does not feel like you are "checking the boxes." A positive handwritten note or company swag such as company shirts or mugs are good ways to show appreciation. If you can, provide lunches on in-office days to create opportunities to connect. Use reunions and holiday parties to get the whole team back together from time to time.

- **Trust your team.** Keep in mind that with the transition, from full-time in-office to a hybrid environment, the traditional work schedule does not necessarily exist. People work when it's convenient for them. Focus on deliverables, not the clock.

- **Temperature check regularly.** Remember that teams, just like individuals, need to have periodic check-ups. Teams cannot afford to be complacent and just assume that everything is going great. As their leader, you can help your team by initiating a quarterly or semi-annual self-examination where the team asks itself questions about goals, customer needs, and how the team is functioning.

Chapter 5: Enduring a Restructuring/Downsizing
Actions for Employees

- **Upskill and reskill.** Build your skills in your current job (upskilling) and learn new cross functional skills for other jobs in your organization (reskilling). Both actions are highly effective in guarding against being the next person to be laid off. Through upskilling and reskilling you will increase your adaptability to change and bring about continuous improvement.

- **Tap your network for people who can help.** Contact people who could be helpful. Sharing your current situation, asking for one additional name, reaching out to these new contacts, and not being shy about asking for their help will expand your network and deepen your relationships.

- **Be aware of the grapevine.** Listen to the rumors, but don't let them incite fear. Remind yourself to remain rational, consider the source, and carefully verify the information with trustworthy sources.

- **Generate your Unique Value Proposition (UVP).** Increase your self-awareness by taking the time to think about how you provide distinct value to your organization, the benefits your organization derives from having you as an employee, and how you differ from other employees. You can create your own UVP by thinking about the answers to the following three questions: (1) Who depends on me the most, and what do they need from me? (2) What skills, knowledge, and wisdom help me meet these needs? and (3) How do I deliver value that makes a real difference?

- **Acknowledge the feelings.** Do not ignore or deny your natural feelings. Only through acknowledging and understanding them can you re-establish your sense of security and fairness. What is important is that you treat your emotions as useful information and find ways to manage them constructively. By doing this, you will increase your level of self-awareness.

- **Consider worst-case scenarios.** Reflect on the "worst-case scenario" and how you would handle it. Doing so will reduce your fear by increasing a sense of control. This process involves thinking about the worst thing that could happen if you were laid off, what you would do if it happened, and the probability that this worst-case scenario could occur. By using this technique, you will increase your positive mindset when faced with all types of change.

Actions for Leaders

- **Use your employee's UVP to advocate.** Tell others in your organization how valuable each of your employees is to the company. Encourage your employees to generate their Unique Value Proposition, working with them to refine it based on your observations. Then, use the UVP as a means of communicating with your own leadership. The UVP will help you provide a crisp message, emphasizing the unique contributions each of your team members makes to the organization.

- **Communicate clearly and often.** Keep your employees informed. This means explaining confidently what has happened, why it's happened, and why your organization is on the right track. It's also important that you find ways to head off rumors among employees and clarify what you expect from each of them from now on.

- **Provide compassionate support.** Provide the employees that stay in the organization with the extra support needed once all the announcements have been made. As the leader, you need to let them know that you realize the hardships imposed on them by the layoffs. It's also essential that you meet with them to give them an opportunity to express their fear, anger, and other feelings. Relationship-building will happen when you show compassion for those employees who are going to have to leave.

- **Restore smart risk-taking.** Keep in mind that layoffs erode trust, performance, and risk-taking. The people who remain with the organization may be especially fearful and reluctant to make a mistake. This can cripple performance. You must tackle this problem proactively and vocally by encouraging your employees to step up while assuring them that they have your support. This is another way to increase relationship-building with your employees.

Chapter 6: Prevailing Through Mergers and Acquisitions

Actions for Employees

- **Adapt to change.** Adjusting to change is critical to your success. Organizational decision-makers should see you as one who adapts well to change no matter where it occurs. To really succeed in the new company, you need to do more than accommodate change. You should be seen as a change agent.

- **Reduce stress.** Adopt techniques such as meditation using the "relaxation response" which has been shown to help reduce stress. Research has shown that those who meditate recover from stress more rapidly than those who do not. Take planned vacations, go to special events that you look forward to, and exercise regularly. And remember, how you *think* will determine how you behave. One thing you can do to change your thinking is to consider the worst-case scenario. Ask yourself, what is the worst possible thing that could happen to me? If you can accept this worst-case scenario, you are on the road to dealing with the situation successfully. You can now put things in perspective, and this will allow you to help maintain a positive mindset.

- **Become part of the solution.** Keep yourself motivated by setting goals, even if you do not know how the M&A will impact you. Use the AIME model for change to help you take steady, intentional steps so that the M&A may feel less overwhelming.

Highlight and reinforce behaviors that will allow you to be a more positive force for change.

- **Stick it out or move on.** Do not psychologically remove yourself from your present position or announce your plans to leave until you have something else lined up. Make sure your productivity remains high. By continually improving on your present job, it also can enhance your skills for your next job. Even if you have already decided to find another job, you are going to need references from your current employer.

- **Get on their wavelength.** Start learning as much as you can about the other company. If you have decided to stay with the organization, make a concerted effort to get to know the other organization. Realize it is time to maintain a positive mindset and start looking for the positive in both the other company and its people. You are all on the same team.

Actions for Leaders

- **Prioritize communication.** Make a conscious decision to communicate more than you think is necessary. Do not exceed the available facts, but make sure you communicate continually, with timely and comprehensive information. Keep in mind that you will likely have to repeat the same important message multiple times for people to digest the content. The more informed employees are, the more positive their attitudes toward the merger will be.

- **Model positive leadership.** Publicize anything the two firms do together. Become a spokesperson for the merger and a role model for a positive attitude. As the leader, you have the greatest impact on what employees will think of the merger and how they will act. Your goal should be to help them let go of the past by getting them enthusiastic about the future.

- **Involve employees.** Ask employees to help design the change. If your department is merging with another, allow your employees to share their ideas about the most effective ways of integrating the teams. Allow departmental employees to collaborate and put together what they consider to be their greatest strengths that will contribute to the success of the new department.

- **Be available.** Serve as a counselor and good listener to show you still value their opinions and ideas. Let the employees know that you realize that fear and anxiety are often an unfortunate byproduct of M&As. Wherever these feelings come from, let your employees know that you are willing to listen and discuss them. You can do this through holding "mini" town halls.

- **Offer dignity and respect.** Remember that how you treat the leavers will affect the stayers. Employees will feel guilty about being "survivors." Make sure that you acknowledge the experience that the stayers bring to the firm. Let them know that you respect and appreciate their years of service and that their experience and expertise will help make the new company more successful.

- **Show empathy.** Be careful about the impression you make with employees from the other company, especially if you are a manager from the acquiring firm. Showing that you understand and are willing to listen to concerns can have a positive effect on how you communicate, how you lead, and ultimately, how successful you are at managing during the M&A.

Chapter 7: Building a Sense of Security Amidst Economic Turmoil

Actions for Employees

- **Focus on your sphere.** Focus on areas where your actions make a difference – such as how you manage your time, respond to challenges, or prioritize your daily activities. Make it explicit and tangible for yourself by, for example, creating a list of the things you can control and influence, and be sure to revisit it regularly to keep your perspective. Channeling your energy into what you can shape strengthens self-management and creates stability, while also empowering you to feel less at the mercy of outside forces.

- **Let go of the things you cannot control.** Notice when you waste energy on issues you can't change – like high-level executive decisions or market fluctuations. When you feel caught up in worry, pause to ask yourself: "What's one action I can take today that's actually within my control?" This is making a conscious choice to redirect your energy. This practice results in greater self-awareness and self-management, while refocusing your effort on controllable actions where your efforts can have an impact.

- **Write your "operating manual."** Take time to reflect on what helps you feel grounded (e.g., routines, healthy habits, collaborative teamwork) and what unsettles you (e.g., last-minute requests, unclear expectations). Reflect on and then write down the things that help you stay effective to make your operating manual more tangible and practical. When you have this level of self-awareness, you can reduce the derailers that can hinder your progress and, consequently, set yourself up for success.

- **Track accomplishments.** Notice the small wins, wherever they are and whenever they occur. Collect small wins by writing them in a notebook, tracking them in app, or sending yourself a voice memo. Set aside a weekly time to review your notes to see progress that might otherwise get lost. Whatever method you choose, having them at hand reinforces a positive mindset and builds confidence. It also supports continuous improvement, since any step forward becomes visible and repeatable.

- **Be fiscally responsible.** Exercise (a little more) control over your finances to increase your sense of ownership. Review your spending, create a small savings buffer, and/or look for low-cost alternatives that ease financial pressure. Start small, such as making one spending cut so the habit becomes achievable and sustainable. Exercising this kind of control demonstrates adaptability to the demands of uncertain times.

- **Expand your options.** Exploring new approaches and possibilities will deepen your sense of ownership. Consider developing new skills, volunteering for stretch assignments, or cultivating new professional connections to broaden your opportunities and exposure. Dedicating as little as 30 minutes a week to a new course, professional group, or project can expand your options over time. It will make you feel more prepared for shifts in your environment.

Actions for Leaders

- **Acknowledge uncertainty through dialogue.** Recognize the stress that economic turmoil can create in your employees instead of letting it go unspoken. Ignoring a difficult topic does not make it better. Even a simple statement like, "I know this is a tough climate," validates employees' feelings, showing empathy without adding drama. Encourage employees to share what part of the uncertainty is most on their minds, then listen actively without rushing to fix it. Raising the topic will strengthen the relationships within your team and help employees manage their uneasiness in constructive ways.

- **Share your experience.** Draw from your own experiences of navigating past downturns or major changes. As a leader, you have likely had your own history with difficult business circumstances. Share specific strategies that have helped you or other senior people to persevere. Employees often gain confidence by seeing that others have faced similar challenges and found ways through them. By role-modeling openness, you foster learning agility and encourage adaptability within your team.

- **Model stability.** Demonstrate steadiness through your words and actions – align what you say with your deeds. Simple behaviors like starting meetings on time, following through on promises, and maintaining a steady tone all signal reliability during turbulent times. When employees see that they can rely on you, it increases their sense of stability and helps them feel more secure. When you do this, you will strengthen their self-management so they can manage the tasks at hand.

- **Use hindsight.** Look back to plan forward. When the present feels unsettled and the future seems uncertain, one of the most effective ways to regain perspective is to look back. Use "Stability Retrospectives" to help employees recall how they've already navigated challenges and persevered. Whether in a team meeting or one-on-one, ask simple reflective questions such as: What stayed the same and what changed over the past 90 days? What did you do that helped you handle those changes? What does that show you about handling the next 90 days? These conversations build self-awareness and adaptability, while reinforcing that your employees can navigate the current challenge.

- **Reaffirm employee's value.** Recognize your employees in specific and meaningful ways, especially during uncertain times. To do this effectively, highlight clear examples of what they did well, emphasize the contributions within their control, and connect their inputs to broader team success. Try giving recognition promptly and in a setting where it will have the most positive impact – in private for reassurance or in public to acknowledge their contribution to the group. This kind of feedback strengthens a positive mindset, fosters ownership, and reinforces a sense of belonging that helps employees feel more secure.

- **Emphasize structure and focus.** Set clear priorities with your employees so that they know what matters most, especially when uncertainty makes it hard to separate urgent topics from the critically important ones. Even simple direction – such as identifying the one project that deserves attention or the task that can be deprioritized – can help your employees gain a sense of clarity and control. Providing structure not only orients them towards the most impactful work but also serves as a calming force that helps employees feel more secure amid economic turmoil.

Chapter 8: Prioritizing Personal Well-Being

Actions for Employees

- **Define your boundaries clearly.** Take ownership of your well-being by knowing your limits so you can stay healthy and effective. Define your boundaries in three areas: (1) personal life (e.g., your availability outside work hours), (2) job responsibilities (e.g., willingness to take on stretch assignments), and (3) interpersonal dynamics (e.g., tone, communication, and respect).

By clarifying these, you increase your self-awareness and self-management for what conditions make you thrive.

- **Maintain your boundaries.** Express your boundaries with clarity and respect. This may feel uncomfortable, but advocating for yourself is a necessary act for you to prioritize your well-being. Let others know what you need, not as a demand, but to stay effective in your role.

- **Respect the boundaries of others.** Just as you want your boundaries honored, demonstrate the same healthy behavior to your colleagues. When you respect others' limits, you normalize healthy boundary-setting across the team.

- **Build your "Wellness Network."** Surround yourself with trusted people who can provide perspective, encouragement, and guidance. This is your "Wellness Network." It can include your peers, confidants, mentors, and coaches, all of whom have your best interest at heart. Having these resources available when stress spikes will help you recover quickly and stay healthy.

- **Develop an exit strategy.** Keep your options open. If you are in an unhealthy work environment, consider leaving your role. Keep your résumé and profile up to date just in case. Preparing in advance gives you greater confidence and flexibility, two essential components of self-management and long-term well-being.

Actions for Leaders

- **Discuss boundaries – theirs and yours.** Learn what boundaries are important to your employees and share what boundaries are important to you. There will very likely be common ground that you can mutually agree on. Respecting employees' private life is essential for well-being. This will improve relationship-building and teamwork.

- **Check-in regularly.** Meet with your employees regularly to find out how they are *feeling*, not just what they are *doing*. When feasible, act on what they say to demonstrate to them your commitment to employee health. This will go a long way in building healthy, sustainable relationships.

- **Watch for warning signs.** Don't ignore the early warning signs – they'll only get worse. Don't wait to open dialogue; meet privately with your employees to work together to diagnose what is causing their loss of personal well-being. This will enhance your employees' positive mindset.

- **Offer guidance on priorities.** Help your employees channel their efforts effectively. Many employees feel that they have too much to do, and not enough time to do it. You can increase your employees' feeling of personal well-being by showing them how to categorize their work activities into those that should be done now, scheduled for later, delegated to others, and eliminated. By doing this with them, you will help them focus and assume greater ownership for their work.

- **Provide resources.** Recommend appropriate wellness programs (e.g., stress management, physical health programs, mental health support, work-life balance programs) to your employees. Keep in mind that they are not sufficient for well-being, but they help to improve resilience and a positive mindset.

- **Model healthy behaviors.** Be aware that your team is watching your behavior. Because of this, as their leader, you need to set an example for your employees on how you want them to behave to create the kind of healthy culture you want. Leaders who do this enhance their employees' positive mindset, learning agility, and continuous improvement.

Concluding Remarks

Choosing actions from the preceding chapters will strengthen your abilities in the **10 Keys for Success**. We believe these 10 Keys will continue to define high performance for both employees and leaders in the turbulent years ahead. The recommended actions are practical, proven techniques to enhance your skills in these 10 critical areas. Strengthening these capabilities will make you more successful and, in turn, strengthen your organization. We hope this book equips you with the skills and confidence to navigate change and achieve success in turbulent times.

Appendix

The 10 Keys for Success Survey

The actions described in this book create distinct opportunities to strengthen your capabilities in the 10 Keys for Success. A useful exercise is for you to describe how you currently believe you're doing on each of the Keys. Take a few minutes to complete the survey by *reading each of the statements and decide how strongly you agree with each description of you.*

	Strongly Disagree	Disagree	Somewhat Agree	Agree	Strongly Agree
Self-Awareness					
I understand what motivates me and why.					
I understand my core values and how they guide my decisions.					
I feel comfortable describing my preferences to others.					
I know how to set myself up for success.					

(continued)

	Strongly Disagree	Disagree	Somewhat Agree	Agree	Strongly Agree
I see that feedback helps me better understand myself, including revealing potential blind-spots.					
I know my strengths and the key areas for growth.					
Self-Management					
I understand my key responsibilities.					
I have a clear understanding of what is expected of me at work.					
I have regular check-ins with my manager to discuss my progress at work.					
I know what I must do to be successful in my key responsibilities.					
I manage my time effectively to maximize my performance.					
I balance my workload and personal well-being to sustain performance.					

	Strongly Disagree	Disagree	Somewhat Agree	Agree	Strongly Agree
Positive Mindset					
I avoid negative self-talk and regularly remind myself of positive things.					
I manage my emotions effectively and channel fear into constructive actions.					
I strive for balance in my life.					
I use stress reduction techniques to maintain my positive energy at work.					
I stay positive at work by focusing on what I can control.					
I look for the best in new situations and in my colleagues.					
Ownership					
I can differentiate the things I control, what I influence, and what is out of my hands.					

(continued)

	Strongly Disagree	Disagree	Somewhat Agree	Agree	Strongly Agree
I make a conscious choice to focus on what I can control.					
I use influencing skills whenever possible to advocate for my needs and interests.					
I recognize that my career progress depends on me taking an active role in my development.					
I take responsibility for the outcomes of my actions.					
Learning Agility					
I look for intentional learning opportunities.					
I acknowledge and learn from my mistakes.					
I welcome candid feedback to improve my performance.					
I seek out new knowledge, skills, and experiences.					

	Strongly Disagree	Disagree	Somewhat Agree	Agree	Strongly Agree
I am receptive to input and ideas from others to help me develop.					
I stay curious and open to fresh ways of thinking.					
Adaptability					
I understand the need for change.					
I encourage and welcome change.					
I recover quickly from setbacks.					
I adapt the way my work is done to create effective outcomes.					
I help others understand the benefits of change.					
I role model adaptability so others can see how to adjust.					
Communication					
I am willing to listen to others' opinions, ideas, or perspectives.					

(continued)

	Strongly Disagree	Disagree	Somewhat Agree	Agree	Strongly Agree
I give feedback to others in a constructive manner.					
I welcome candid feedback about myself.					
I reflect on how my message might impact others.					
I tailor my communication style to the audience.					
I communicate information clearly.					
I solicit feedback to ensure my message is understood.					
Relationship Building					
I treat others with courtesy and respect.					
I am open, honest, and direct in dealing with others.					
I am trusted by my colleagues.					
I relate well to all levels of the organization.					

	Strongly Disagree	Disagree	Somewhat Agree	Agree	Strongly Agree
I get work done while maintaining positive interpersonal relationships.					
I proactively expand my network beyond my immediate team.					
Teamwork					
I help others work more effectively as a team.					
I am a consistent contributor to the team's mission and goals.					
I help celebrate team accomplishments.					
I acknowledge others for good team behavior.					
I encourage collaboration and promote a cooperative team environment.					
I address disagreements constructively to maintain team cohesion.					

(continued)

	Strongly Disagree	Disagree	Somewhat Agree	Agree	Strongly Agree
I participate effectively as a team member – and others recognize me for my collaborative style.					
Continuous Improvement					
I look for ways to make small, constant, incremental improvements in my work.					
I am not satisfied with the status quo; I seek and act on opportunities to improve my performance.					
I do not rely solely on the proven methods of the past.					
I seek out and apply new technology, knowledge, and skills.					
I am willing to experiment and learn with new ways of doing things.					

	Strongly Disagree	Disagree	Somewhat Agree	Agree	Strongly Agree
I am committed to improving so I maintain an action plan for my personal development.					
I monitor and acknowledge my progress to ensure improvements are sustained.					

Scoring the 10 Keys for Success Survey

Review your answers across the 10 Keys. Note any item above where you answered "Strongly Agree" or "Agree." These are sources of strength that can support you during turbulent times. Leverage them by continuing to focus on them.

Now let's turn to the other end of the scale. Wherever you selected "Strongly Disagree," "Disagree," or "Somewhat," it indicates an area for your professional development.

Which results surprised you?

Which results concern you?

Which results matter to you most? And why?

If you are interested in maximizing your success in your current job, which of the 10 Keys are most critical for you to work on? Below is a technique to create an action plan.

Creating an Action Plan

- Assess how the 10 Keys are related to your current key job responsibilities and future career growth. List your responsibilities along with the 10 Keys to success. Which keys are most important to your current role and which keys are most important to your future career goals?

- Conduct a review and analysis of your survey results to identify your strengths and areas for improvement. After reviewing the 10 Keys to success survey, identify which keys are strengths, and which keys show there is room for development.

- Discuss your results with your manager and several select peers which keys you believe will be a development focus for you.

- Develop an effective action plan. Look for behavioral strategies, activities, and readings for developing on those specific keys.

- Implement your action plan and evaluate your progress.

Acknowledgments

We owe a great deal of thanks to the many people who agreed to share their stories and experiences with us. It takes courage to admit to being afraid. Many of them asked us not to reveal their companies – out of fear – but they felt compelled to share their story. To those individuals, you know who you are. We will always be grateful to you for the time you gave us and enduring the discomfort in relaying your experiences.

We also owe a great deal of thanks to the following people:

Steve Abseck, consultant in financial services; Debra Evans-Holmes, project manager; Sandy Goel, PharmD, Go Well Advisory; Adam Goldfarb, Manco Abbott, Inc.; Michael Goldfarb, Manco Abbott, Inc.; Lindsay Goodman, Sprout Social, Inc.; Mike Goodman, James Hardie Industries; Tünde Horváth, leadership and team coach and founder of Space to Adapt; Adam Nathan, AI solutions engineer; "R.S." researcher at the National Institutes of Health; Ryan Silverman, Albertsons Companies, Inc.; Max Wexley, financial analyst in the energy sector.

Last, but never least, we'd like to say thanks to our families. They had to tolerate our feelings of "writing scared" as we struggled to gather our thoughts and commit them to paper, while meeting our editors' schedule. Special thanks to Jeanenne Ray, Associate Publisher at Wiley for encouraging us from the very beginning. We also want to thank Michelle Hacker, Raven Buckner, and the entire Wiley team for being so professional.

With love and thanks,
Stanley B. Silverman
Akron, Ohio

Kenneth N. Wexley
Annapolis, Maryland

David H. Wexley
New York, New York
January 2026

The Authors

Stanley B. Silverman

Stan Silverman is Dean Emeritus and Professor Emeritus at The University of Akron and President of Human Resource Decisions, Inc. He has advised organizations of all sizes, including some of the world's largest companies, on leadership development, organizational change, performance management, and talent development. His clients have included General Motors, Moen, Bridgestone/Firestone, and Allstate.

Stan has co-authored books and numerous articles on performance appraisal, personnel selection, and employee development in leading journals such as *The Journal of Applied Psychology* and *Personnel Psychology*. He has been active nationally with the Society for Industrial and Organizational Psychology and co-authored a book chapter that received the 2010 HRD Book of the Year Award. His research on arrogance in the workplace has been widely cited, and he has presented his work internationally.

A frequent speaker across the United States and Europe, Stan has appeared on national radio and television, including NBC's *Today Show*. He was recently recognized as one of the most influential Industrial and Organizational Psychologists alive today. In 2022, he was inducted into the Cleveland Heights High School Distinguished Alumni Hall of Fame (stanley@uakron.edu).

Kenneth N. Wexley

Kenneth Wexley is founder and CEO of Wexley Consulting, an internationally recognized firm specializing in leadership development, organizational effectiveness, and performance management. Since earning his Ph.D. in Industrial and Organizational Psychology, Ken has become widely known as a consultant, author, lecturer, and researcher.

Ken has advised hundreds of organizations across industries on organizational change, leadership development, staffing, and strategic planning. He has published more than 100 professional articles and co-authored 11 books. His academic career has included professorships at the University of California–Berkeley, the University of Akron, Michigan State University, and the University of Sheffield in England.

He has been recognized as a Fellow of the American Psychological Association and a Charter Fellow of the Association for Psychological Science for his contributions to the field. Ken has also served on the editorial boards of several leading journals and is a sought-after speaker in the United States and internationally (ken@wexleyconsulting.com).

David H. Wexley

David Wexley is President of Wexley Consulting. David is an experienced organizational consultant and executive coach specializing in change leadership and cross-cultural team collaboration. With more than 25 years of global experience, he has partnered with leaders across six continents to design and implement large-scale transformation initiatives.

David has held senior executive positions with Siemens AG and worked as a strategy consultant at Siemens Management Consulting and Booz Allen Hamilton. His work at Siemens Healthineers included leading post-merger integrations and organizational change initiatives affecting more than 70,000 employees across 75+ countries.

As a consultant, he has advised FTSE100, S&P500, and entrepreneurial companies on aligning leadership and organizational effectiveness with business objectives.

Known as a "cultural bridge-builder," David is recognized for helping leaders create environments where diverse perspectives translate into impactful action. He earned an MBA with distinction from Columbia Business School, an Executive Master's in Change from INSEAD, a master's from Johns Hopkins School of Advanced International Studies (SAIS), and a bachelor's with high honors from the University of Michigan. He is certified through the International Coach Federation and the NeuroLeadership Institute, with advanced training in leadership excellence, team effectiveness, and organizational transformation (david@wexleyconsulting.com).

Notes

Chapter 1: Adapting to a Changing Workplace

1. PricewaterhouseCoopers. (n.d.). Global Workforce Hopes and Fears Survey 2024. PwC. https://www.pwc.com/gx/en/issues/workforce/hopes-and-fears.html
2. O Morain, C., & Aykens, P. (2023). Employees Are Losing Patience with Change Initiatives. Harvard Business Review.
3. Barrett, H., & Kemp, A. (2024, May 23). Disruptive Change Is Hitting Leaders and Managers Hardest. Gallup. https://www.gallup.com/workplace/645152/disruptive-change-hitting-leaders-managers-hardest.aspx
4. World Economic Forum. (2025). Future of Jobs Report 2025. In Insight Report. https://www.weforum.org/reports/the-future-of-jobs-report-2025/
5. Shee, P. Y., Dollard, M. F., & Idris, M. A. (2025). How psychosocial safety climate affects employee well-being via basic psychological needs: A longitudinal multilevel moderated mediation study. *Journal of Applied Psychology*. https://doi.org/10.1037/apl0001304

Chapter 2: Succeeding Amidst Arrogant Leadership

1. Gibbs, N. (2009, November 9). The case for modesty, in an age of arrogance. TIME. https://time.com/archive/6689902/the-case-for-modesty-in-an-age-of-arrogance/
2. Gallup, Inc. (2025, May 7). Employee Wellbeing. https://www.gallup.com/topic/employee-wellbeing.aspx

3. Silverman, S. B., Johnson, R. E., McConnell, N., & Carr, A. (2012). Arrogance: A formula for leadership failure. *The Industrial-Organizational Psychologist*, 50(1), 21–28.
4. Johnson, R. E., Silverman, S. B., Shyamsunder, A., Swee, H., Rodopman, O. B., Cho, E., & Bauer, J. (2010). Acting superior but actually inferior?: Correlates and consequences of workplace arrogance. *Human Performance*, 23(5), 403–427. https://doi.org/10.1080/08959285.2010.515279
5. Gallup. (2025). "75% of Why People Quit Comes Down to Their Leader or Manager. Leadership Matters." LinkedIn, February 10, 2025. https://www.linkedin.com/company/gallup
6. Gallup. (2025). "Great Detachment at Work: Why 51% of U.S. Employees Are Seeking New Jobs." Economic Times HR World, March 5, 2025. https://hrme.economictimes.indiatimes.com/news/industry/great-detachment-at-work-why-51-of-us-employees-are-seeking-new-jobs/118732847
7. Namie, Gary. (2024). *2024 U.S. Workplace Bullying Survey: The Complete Report*. Workplace Bullying Institute. https://workplacebullying.org/wp-content/uploads/2024/10/2024-Complete-Report.pdf
8. Silverman, S. B., Johnson, R. E., McConnell, N., & Carr, A. (2012). Arrogance: A formula for leadership failure [Dataset]. In PsycEXTRA Dataset. https://doi.org/10.1037/e520222013-002
9. Borden, L., Levy, P. E., & Silverman, S. B. (2018). Leader arrogance and subordinate outcomes: The role of feedback processes. *Journal of Business and Psychology*, 33(3), 345–364. https://doi.org/10.1007/s10869-017-9501-1
10. Korn Ferry. (2025, May). *Workforce 2025 Global Insights Report*. Korn Ferry. https://www.theglobalrecruiter.com/korn-ferry-reveals-workforce-2025-research/
11. Gallup. (2024). State of the Global Workplace: 2024 Report. Gallup. https://workplacebullying.org/wp-content/uploads/2024/10/2024-Complete-Report.pdf
12. Harvard Business Impact. (2025). 2025 Global Leadership Development Study. In Harvard Business Impact.

13. Grant, A., & Grant, A. (2025, August 16). The 10 new leadership Books to wrap up summer and kick off Fall. https://www.linkedin.com/in/adammgrant/
14. Miller, M. (2025, May). Understand the importance of role clarity: Leadership insights from 25 years of research and $10M investment [LinkedIn post]. LinkedIn. https://www.linkedin.com/in/markmillerleadership/
15. Silverman, S. B., & Muller, W. M. (2009). Assessing performance management programs and policies. In J. Smithers & M. London (Eds.), *Performance Management: Putting Research into Action* (pp. 527–554). Jossey-Bass.
16. Silverman, S. (2019, June 17). *Why arrogance could be hurting your organization.* Psychology Today. https://www.psychologytoday.com/us/blog/cutting-edge-leadership/201906/why-arrogance-could-be-hurting-your-organization
17. Yip, J., & Fisher, C. M. (2025, May–June). Are You Really a Good Listener? (2025, May 1). Harvard Business Review. https://hbr.org/2025/05/are-you-really-a-good-listener
18. Empathy Is a Core Leadership Skill. (2025, May 5). Harvard Business Review. https://hbr.org/tip/2025/05/empathy-is-a-core-leadership-skill
19. Hayes, E. (2025, May 9). The Small Actions That Become Your Legacy. Harvard Business Review. https://hbr.org/2025/05/the-small-actions-that-become-your-legacy
20. Brown, B. (2018). *Dare to Lead.* Random House. https://www.randomhousebooks.com/books/557595/
21. Borden, L., Levy, P. E., & Silverman, S. B. (2018). Leader arrogance and subordinate outcomes: The role of feedback processes. *Journal of Business and Psychology, 33*(3), 345–364. https://doi.org/10.1007/s10869-017-9501-1
22. Johnson, Russell E., et al. (2010) "Acting superior but actually inferior?: Correlates and consequences of workplace arrogance." *Human Performance, 23*(5), 403–427. https://doi.org/10.1080/08959285.2010.515279

Chapter 3: Amplifying Your Voice in a Team Culture

1. Morrison, E. W., & Milliken, F. J. (2000). Organizational silence: A barrier to change and development in a pluralistic world. *Academy of Management Review*, 25(4), 706. https://doi.org/10.2307/259200
2. Detert, J. R., & Edmondson, A. C. (2011). Implicit voice theories: Taken-for-Granted rules of Self-Censorship at work. *Academy of Management Journal*, 54(3), 461–488. https://doi.org/10.5465/amj.2011.61967925
3. Number of jobs, labor market experience, marital status, and health for those born 1957–1964 – 2022 A01 results. (2023). In Bureau of Labor Statistics. Bureau of Labor Statistics. https://www.bls.gov/news.release/nlsoy.nr0.htm
4. Nica, B. (2025, May 29). Psychological safety and accountability: Three insights from NLI's conversation with Amy Edmondson. NeuroLeadership Institute. https://neuroleadership.com/your-brain-at-work/psychological-safety-and-accountability-insights-from-amy-edmondson
5. *What is Psychological Safety?* (2023, July 17). McKinsey & Company. https://www.mckinsey.com/featured-insights/mckinsey-explainers/what-is-psychological-safety
6. Yousif, N., Dartnell, A., May, G., & Knarr, E. (2025, July 28). Psychological safety levels the playing field for employees. BCG Global. https://www.bcg.com/publications/2024/psychological-safety-levels-playing-field-for-employees
7. Morrison, E. W., & Milliken, F. J. (2000). Organizational silence: a barrier to change and development in a pluralistic world. *Academy of Management Review*, 25(4), 706. https://doi.org/10.2307/259200

Chapter 4: Thriving in a Hybrid Team

1. Global Poll Shows People to Generally be Happy and Optimistic for 2025 . . . yet Economic Hesitancy Remains. (2025, January 28). https://www.gallup-international.com/survey-results-and-news/survey-result/

global-l-shows-people-to-generally-be-happy-and-optimistic-for-2025-yet-economic-hesitancy-remains
2. Massachusetts Institute of Technology. (2024b, June 20). When hybrid work strategy aggravates 20-Somethings | Brian Elliott and Amanda Schneider | MIT Sloan Management Review. MIT Sloan Management Review. https://sloanreview.mit.edu/article/when-hybrid-work-strategy-aggravates-20-somethings/
3. The surprising science of meetings: Lead your team to peak performance – Steven Rogelberg, Ph.D. (n.d.). Steven Rogelberg, Ph.D. https://www.stevenrogelberg.com/the-surprising-science-of-meetings-1
4. Massachusetts Institute of Technology. (2024b, June 20). When hybrid work strategy aggravates 20-Somethings | Brian Elliott and Amanda Schneider | MIT Sloan Management Review. MIT Sloan Management Review. https://sloanreview.mit.edu/article/when-hybrid-work-strategy-aggravates-20-somethings/
5. Cappelli, P., & Nehmeh, R. (2025, July 1). Hybrid Still Isn't Working. Harvard Business Review. https://hbr.org/2025/07/hybrid-still-isnt-working

Chapter 5: Enduring a Restructuring/Downsizing

1. Job Openings and Labor Turnover Survey News Release – 2025 M06 results. (2025, July 29). Bureau of Labor Statistics. https://www.bls.gov/news.release/archives/jolts_07292025.htm#
2. Elzinga, D., & Lavoie, A. (2024, October 9). Research: The Long-Term Costs of Layoffs. Harvard Business Review. https://hbr.org/2024/10/research-the-long-term-costs-of-layoffs
3. Nix, N. (2023, January 30). After layoffs, Meta, tech companies face uphill battle to boost diversity. The Washington Post. https://www.washingtonpost.com/technology/2023/01/27/diversity-layoffs-meta-facebook/
4. Nix, N., Tiku, N., & Thadani, T. (2025, May 19). Big Tech takes a harder line against worker activism, political dissent. The Washington Post. https://www.washingtonpost.com/technology/2025/05/16/silicon-valley-workers-dissent-employment-layoffs-whistleblowers/

5. Elzinga, D., & Lavoie, A. (2024, October 9). Research: The Long-Term Costs of Layoffs. Harvard Business Review. https://hbr.org/2024/10/research-the-long-term-costs-of-layoffs
6. Fosslien, L., & Gottlieb-Cohen, S. (2023, March 22). Research: Remote Workers Are More Anxious About Layoffs. Harvard Business Review. https://hbr.org/2023/03/research-remote-workers-are-more-anxious-about-layoffs

Chapter 6: Prevailing Through Mergers and Acquisitions

1. Henry, J., & Van Oostende, M. (2025). *M&A Annual Report: Is the Wave Finally Arriving?* McKinsey & Company.
2. Mirvis, P. H. and Marks, M. L. (1992). *Managing the Merger: Making It Work.* Prentice-Hall.
3. Mitchell, M., MD. (2013, March 29). Learn to counteract the physiological effects of stress. Psychology Today. https://www.psychologytoday.com/us/blog/heart-and-soul-healing/201303/dr-herbert-benson-s-relaxation-response
4. Ratanjee, V. (2025, April 1). M&A Success Rate Rises to 70% - But Firms Must Navigate 7 Potential Missteps. Forbes. https://www.forbes.com/sites/vibhasratanjee/2025/04/01/ma-success-rate-rises-to-70-but-firms-must-navigate-7-essential-missteps/
5. Ibid.

Chapter 7: Building a Sense of Security Amidst Economic Turmoil

1. American Psychological Association. (2025). 2025 Work in America Survey: The Experience of Working in America during Times of Change. https://www.apa.org/pubs/reports/work-in-america/2025/full-report-working-times-change

2. Board of Governors of the Federal Reverse System. (2025). Economic Well-Being of U.S. Households in 2024. https://www.federalreserve.gov/publications/files/2024-report-economic-well-being-us-households-202505.pdf
3. Deloitte Global Gen Z and Millennial Survey 2025. (2025, May 14). Deloitte. https://www.deloitte.com/global/en/issues/work/genz-millennial-survey.html
4. Adapted from Covey, S. R. (1990). *The Seven Habits of Highly Effective People: Restoring the Character Ethic.* Free Press.

Chapter 8: Prioritizing Personal Well-Being

1. United States. Public Health Service. Surgeon General. (2025, March 13). Workplace Mental Health & Well-Being. HHS.gov. https://www.hhs.gov/surgeongeneral/reports-and-publications/workplace-well-being/index.html
2. *What is burnout?* (2023, August 14). McKinsey & Company. https://www.mckinsey.com/featured-insights/mckinsey-explainers/what-is-burnout
3. Gallup, Inc. (2025). State of the Global Workplace: 2025 Report. In Gallup.com. https://www.gallup.com/workplace/349484/state-of-the-global-workplace.aspx
4. Employee health survey health on demand. (2021). https://www.mercer.com/en-us/insights/total-rewards/employee-benefits-strategy/employee-health-survey-health-on-demand/
5. Global mental health crisis hits workplaces. (2024, December 16). Financial Times.
6. Goel. S. (2025a, April). Don't underestimate your greatness or ignore your well-being: My workplace well-being and leadership lessons learned during the pandemic. Linkedin.
7. Goel, S. (2025b, May). The Workplace Well-Being Accountability Gap. DailyDose.Business on Linkedin.
8. Goel. S. (2025c, January 21). Beating burnout: Dr. Sandy Goel of Go Well Advisory on the 5 things you should do if you are experiencing work burnout. Medium-Authority Magazine.

9. Adapted from Stephen R. Covey, *The Seven Habits of Highly Effective People: Restoring the Character Ethic* (Free Press, 1990).
10. Grant, R. S., Buchanan, B. E., & Shockley, K. M. (2025). I need a vacation: A meta-analysis of vacation and employee well-being. *Journal of Applied Psychology.* https://doi.org/10.1037/apl0001262

Index

acceptance zones, 126–127
Advisory Committee, 13
AI. *See* artificial intelligence
AIME. *See* Align, Integrate, Monitor, and Elevate (AIME)
Align, Integrate, Monitor, and Elevate (AIME) Model, 7, 13–16, 115, 131, 161–163, 177
align stage, 8–9, 161–162
anchor days, 79–80, 173
arrogant leadership. *See* workplace arrogance
artificial intelligence (AI), 4–5, 9–13, 15, 18–19
authentic communication, 157
authentic leadership, 18–19, 164

Benson, Herbert, 111
boundaries, personal, 144–146, 150, 183–184
build learning agility, 157

communication norms, 79, 172–173
compassionate support, 97, 176

confidante's network, 147
conquering heroes, 109, 121–122
continuous improvement, 158
control zones, 126–127, 180
co-workers changing, 108
cross-functional relationships, 72–73, 172
cultivate teamwork, 158
culture clash stage, 105–106

decision-making style, 80–81
development opportunities, 64–65, 170–171
disruptive changes, 2, 127
downsizing/restructuring organization, xiii, 85–86
  communicating information, 96–97, 176
  compassionate support, 97, 176
  reskilling, 87–88, 174
  risk-taking, 97, 176–177
  rumors, 89–90, 175
  seeking support, 88, 175
  thoughts and feelings, 92–93, 175
  upskilling, 87–88, 174

downsizing/restructuring
organization (*continued*)
and UVP, 90–92, 95–96, 176
worst case scenario, 94, 175–176

economic uncertainty, xiii, 123–124
acceptance zone, 126–127
acknowledging, 135–136, 181–182
contributions, 129
control zone, 126–127, 180
fiscal responsibility, 132–133, 181
flexibility, 133–134, 181
influence zone, 126–127, 180
investing development, 128–129, 181
operating manual, 129–131, 180
personal habits control, 127–128
practical knowledge, 136, 182
professional development, 128–129, 181
reinforcing employee's value, 138–139, 183
Stability Retrospectives, 136–138, 182
structure and focus, 139–140, 183
tracking values, 131–132, 180–181
Eisenhower Matrix. *See* Prioritization Matrix
elevation stage, 13–14, 162
emerging stage, 106
enhance employee appreciation, 78–79, 174

enhance self-management, 156
exhibit leadership, 120
exit strategy, 148–149, 184
Eyes and Ears First approach, 54, 65

fiscal responsibility, 132–133, 181
5W framework, 56–57, 168
force stabilization, 164

Gallup survey, 77
Gallup workforce indicators, 25–26
goal-setting process, 116
Grant, Adam, 32
grief stages, 114–115

Harvard Medical School, 111
hybrid work environment, xii–xiii, 67–68
cross-functional relationships, 72–73, 171–172
empathetic leadership, 75
enhance appreciation, 78–79, 174
in-person meetings, 78, 173
leverage technology, 76–77, 172
open communications, 73–75, 172
periodic check-ups, 83, 174
return-to-office policy, 79, 173
seeking support, 71–72, 171
segmenting work time, 75–76, 172
norms and expectations, 79, 82–83, 173

tracking progress, 71, 171
trusting team, 77, 80–83, 172–174
using anchor days, 79–80, 173
using collaboration platforms, 76–77, 173

influence zones, 126–127, 180
in-office relationship, 72–73, 171–172
in-person team meetings, 78, 173
intangible signs progress, 12
integration stage, 9–10, 162
interaction principles, 64, 170
Intro to AI for Business Professionals, 11
investing development, 128–129, 181

key job responsibilities, 33–34, 165
Key Performance Indicators (KPIs), 5, 19, 21, 22, 165
vs micro-Performance Indicators (mPIs), 23
KPIs. *See* Key Performance Indicators
Kübler–Ross, Elisabeth, 114–115

layoffs. *See* downsizing/restructuring organization
leadership attributes, 42, 167
leverage relationships, 158
leverage technology, 76, 172

McKinsey study reports, 51, 104
mentor's network, 147–148
mergers and acquisitions (M&As), xiii, 103–106. *See also* workplace changes
co-worker's changes, 108
dignity and respect, 121, 179
exhibit leadership, 120
organizational culture changes, 106–107, 177
positive leadership, 119–120, 178–179
prioritize communication, 119, 178
role changes, 107–108
stress and uncertainty, 109–118
merging stage, 106
micro-Performance Indicators (mPIs), 19, 21, 22, 164–165
vs Key Performance Indicators (KPIs), 23
mindset shifts, 19, 55, 136
model healthy behaviors, 153–154, 185
monitoring stage, 11–13, 19
mPIs. *See* micro-Performance Indicators

official news drops stage, 105
one-on-one (1:1) meetings, 71, 78, 171
operating manual, 129–131, 180

organizational culture changes, 106–107, 177
organizational silence, 50

peer's network, 146–147
perceived risk, 50, 59, 169
performance expectations, 35–37
periodic check-ins, 83, 150–151, 174, 185
personal well-being, xiv, 141
    boundaries, 144–146, 150, 183–184
    exit strategy, 148–149, 184
    model healthy behaviors, 153–154, 185
    periodic check-ins, 150–151, 185
    prioritizing activities, 151–152, 185
    resources, 153, 185
    return-on-investment (ROI), 149
    warning signs, 151, 185
    Wellness Network, 146–148, 184
pharmaceutical company, 3, 11, 12, 19, 31
positive leadership, 119–120, 178–179
positive mindset, 156, 162, 165, 176–178, 181, 183, 185
potential reward, 59
practice adaptability, 157
preoccupation stage, 105
Prioritization Matrix, 152
professional development, 128–129, 181
psychological safety, 18, 50–51, 164

real-world coaching engagements, 148
reductions in force. *See* downsizing/restructuring organization
relaxation response, 111, 177
reskilling efforts, 87–88, 174
return-on-investment (ROI), 149
return-to-office (RTO) policies, 68, 79, 173
ripple effects, 40
risk–reward calculus, 59–60, 169
ROI. *See* return-on-investment
role ambiguity, 93
role clarity, 33, 167–168
RTO. *See* return-to-office
rumours, 89–90, 175

segmenting work time, 75–76, 172
self-awareness, development, 156
sense of security, uncertainty, xiii, 123–124
    acceptance zone, 126–127
    acknowledging, uncertainty, 135–136, 181–182
    contributions, 129
    control zone, 126–127, 180
    fiscal responsibility, 132–133, 181
    flexibility, 133–134, 181
    influence zone, 126–127, 180
    investing development, 128–129
    operating manual, 129–131, 180
    personal habits control, 126–127
    practical knowledge, 136, 182

professional development, 128–129, 181
reinforcing employee's value, 138–139, 183
Stability Retrospectives, 136–138, 182
structure and focus, 139–140, 183
tracking values, 131–132, 180–181
skill sets
  adaptability, 16–17, 163–164
  improving, 87
  new cross-functional, 88
  upskill and reskill, 87–88
Slack Messaging, 76, 79, 172
smart risk-taking, 98, 176–177
speaking up, workplace, 49–50, 52–53
  culture of voice, 60–63, 169, 170
  development opportunities, 64–65, 170–171
  encourage contribution, 63, 170
  5W framework, 56–57, 168–169
  interaction principles, 64, 170
  mindset shift to, 55–56
  observe and listen, 53–54, 168
  risk–reward calculus, 59–60, 169
  trusted circle, 57–58, 169
Stability Retrospectives, 136, 182
supervisory responsibilities, 112

tangible indicators, 12–13
team culture, xii, 49–51
  healthy, 146, 153
  in-person, meetings, 78, 173
  norms and expectations, 79, 173
  personal well-being, 149, 153
  reinforce healthy, 146
  speaking up. See speaking up, workplace
team trust, 17, 80–83, 174
Teams Messaging, 76, 79, 172
10 Keys for Success Survey, 155–161, 186–196
360° development process, 30, 41–43, 167
tracking progress, 71, 171
transparent communication, 164
turbulent situations, 155–161

Unique Value Proposition (UVP), 90–92, 99–101, 175
upskilling efforts, 87–88, 174
UVP. See Unique Value Proposition

Wellness Network, 146, 184
wellness resources, 153
work-life balance programs, 153
workplace arrogance, xii, 25–26, 47–48
  consequences, 26–30
  control issues, 31
  feedback, 33–39, 44–45, 166–168
  key responsibilities, 33–34, 38, 165
  performance expectations, 31, 35–38
  relationship with manager, 32–33

workplace arrogance (*continued*)
   ripple effect, 40–41
   role clarity, 33, 167–168
   self-confidence, 26
   self-perception, 30
   360° process, 41–43, 167
   willingness to listen, 43–44, 167
Workplace Arrogance
   Scale, 27, 46–47
workplace changes, xii, 1–3
   aligning goal, 8–9, 161–162
   authentic leadership, 18–19
   co-worker changes, 108
   creating space, dialogue, 17–18
   elevation stage, 13–14, 162
   fear managing
      technique, 6–7, 161
   integration stage, 9–11, 162
   monitoring progress, 11–13, 162
   organizational culture, 107
   psychological safety, 18, 164
   role changes, 107–108
   skill sets, 16–17, 163
   stress and uncertainty, 109–114
   team trust, 17
   using AIME framework, 15–16, 163–165
   using mPIs, 19–20, 164
workplace stress, 177
   catastrophizing, 113
   grief, 114–115
   management programs, 153
   managing stress
      techniques, 111–114
   overgeneralization, 112
   positive self-talk, 113
   reduction techniques, 153
   selective perception, 112
   setting goals, 115–118
   visualize your actions, 114
worst-case scenario, 94, 113, 175–177